Wisdom With Understanding is Better Than Rubies

Lurine Karon Greenberg Fine Arts Collection

THE ULTIMATE

BEER LOVER'S

COOKBOOK

The Ultimate

Beer Lover's

Cookbook

More Than 400 Recipes

Compiled, Edited, & Introduced By

John Schlimm

Cumberland House
Nashville, Tennessee

The Ultimate Beer Lover's Cookbook
Published by Cumberland House Publishing, Inc.
431 Harding Industrial Drive
Nashville, TN 37211-3160

Copyright © 2008 by John E. Schlimm II

Permission to use the excerpt of "A Hymn to the Beer Goddess and a Drinking Song" from *Studies Presented to A. Leo Oppenheim,* edited by Robert D. Biggs and John A. Brinkman, translated by Miguel Civil, generously granted by The Oriental Institute of The University of Chicago.

Cover design: Bruce Gore
Text design: Julie Pitkin

Library of Congress Cataloging-in-Publication Data

Schlimm, John E., 1971-
   The ultimate beer lover's cookbook : more than 400 recipes / compiled, edited & introduced by John E. Schlimm II.
       p. cm.
   Includes index.
   ISBN-13: 978-1-58182-651-7 (hardcover) : alk. paper)
   ISBN-10: 1-58182-651-6 (hardcover) : alk. paper)
   1. Cookery (Beer) I. Title.

TX726.3.S38 2008
641.6'23--dc22

                              2008008306

Printed in the United States of America
2 3 4 5 6 7—14 13 12 11 10 09 08

To My Mom & Dad,
and, of course, Little Coyote

"...YOU LUSTY GOLDEN BREW, WHOEVER IMBIBES TAKES FIRE FROM YOU. THE YOUNG AND THE OLD SING YOUR PRAISES; HERE'S TO BEER, HERE'S TO CHEER, HERE'S TO BEER."

Bedrich Smetana, from *The Bartered Bride*

CONTENTS

ACKNOWLEDGMENTS

When you're working with a global superstar that is more than 7,000 years old, there's going to naturally be a millennia's worth of people to thank—Sumerian women, a few thousand Mesopotamians and Babylonians, Chinese villagers, ancient Greeks and Romans, Egyptian pharaohs, some kings, queens, and barbarians from the Middle Ages, tribes of Native Americans, a Founding Father or two, a great-great-grandfather who happened to launch an award-winning brewery in the 1870s, and so on.
Beer lovers of history, you know who you are and only you know the hard work and sweat you put into making beer the international icon it is today.

So, I will reserve the bulk of my acknowledgment page for the 21st Century and those whose efforts are most directly linked to the fate of the cookbook you now hold in your hands.

A million thank you's to my publisher, Ron Pitkin, at Cumberland House Publishing. He is a true visionary and treasure within the book industry. My deepest gratitude also to my tireless editor extraordinaire, Julie Pitkin, an accomplished cookbook author and editor in her own right, as well as being the other half of this dynamic publishing power couple.

As a former publicist, I, better than most, know the hard work and dedication Paige Lakin has put into this cookbook. Publicists are often the masterminds behind-the-scenes, making sure the author is seen and heard. I am forever grateful for the poise, grace, and pure elbow grease Paige and the publicity team at Cumberland House has put into this project.

My applause also goes out to the amazing Marketing Department at Cumberland House Publishing, headed by Chris Bauerle. It is thanks to these men and women that you were able to buy this cookbook at your favorite store or web site. My thanks to Brian Ellsworth and the sales and marketing staff.

Although we're taught to never judge a book by its cover, luckily for this cookbook, doing just that is a safe and ultimately pallet-pleasing bet. My thanks to Bruce Gore for this cover design.

One of the things I like most about Cumberland House Publishing is how everyone there works together as a team to produce the best books possible. My thanks to all of the individuals who help make Cumberland House a First Class company all the way.

On the home front, I am blessed to be surrounded by an amazing team of advisors and friends (I certainly didn't have to look far for willing taste testers!), whose collective input into this project was invaluable. These individuals include my parents, Jack and Barb Schlimm, who are two marvelous cooks; Steven K. Troha, who is one of the literary world's best power publicists and my best friend; Patty Burden, one of my most trusted culinary advisors; everyone at Straub Brewery, Inc.; and many more. And, to anyone my mind and pen have forgotten, please know that my heart never forgets.

Finally, my absolute, positively, without a doubt BIGGEST thank you goes to the millions of fellow beer lovers around the world. This book is first and foremost for you because, like the vibe of this book, you have always known that BEER = FUN!

May you always be able to eat, drink, and laugh to your heart's content.

INTRODUCTION

By John Schlimm

"From man's sweat and God's love, beer came into the world. "

SAINT ARNOLD, THE PATRON SAINT OF BREWERS

THE GOLDEN ROCK STAR

When I set out to create *The Ultimate Beer Lover's Cookbook* more than a decade ago, I had one goal in mind: To throw the ultimate party in a book. This became an easy task once I realized I was working with the most popular and beloved thirst quencher of all time, a true international superstar of bar and screen. The beer party I planned to throw would be a 24 hour, 365 day brew fest across the globe.

From the minute beer lovers get up in the morning for breakfast until they munch on that midnight snack, I was determined that beer would take them on an unforgettable joyride. This would be the only four letter word they'd ever need, to get through the day with a smile on their face and a tingle on their pallet.

As one of my friends likes to say, BEER = FUN. That's what this book is intended to be. 100% pure grade FUN.

Consider *The Ultimate Beer Lover's Cookbook* your all-access pass to the event of the season, and allow me the honor of *re*introducing you to a bona fide legend like you've never seen it before.

Beer is the ultimate rock star of the culinary world. Boasting worldwide sales of nearly $300 billion annually, this hearty concoction of barley, hops, yeast, and other earthy ingredients has dominated the ultra-competitive food and beverage circuit for millennia.

It has history, style, and charisma on its side, not to mention a fan base that numbers well into the hundreds of millions of the partying faithful. It appears nonstop across the globe, headlining at bars, restaurants, casinos, campgrounds, homes, frat houses, sold-out stadiums, and at its very own museums. It's a true media bonanza, having starred in countless songs, books, movies, television shows, video games, and on billboards, often leaving its carbonated and fruity competition in the dust. Beer has also had countless royal audiences (Queen Elizabeth I was a hug fan, drinking ale for breakfast), and even rolls with its own posse of gods, goddesses, and patron saints!

Whether kegged, bottled, canned, free flowing, or whipped into a batch of scrambled eggs, this consummate A-Lister never fails to attract attention and please the thirsty and ravenous masses. Its bobbing and weaving between sweet and bitter and smooth styles demonstrates a versatile performer that can help one drown the blues or score big time.

The good ol' brewski is the favored toast of holiday gatherings, summer picnics, and its very own worldwide festivals, as well as weddings, bar mitzvahs, Super Bowl blow-outs, 21st birthdays, and even the occasional funeral. In the end, every sip, gulp, or chugging of this ageless delight is all about friendship, laughter, and celebrating life to the absolute fullest.

Beer has also been involved in some tabloid-worthy run-ins, as would be expected of any hard partying rock star. And I'm not just referring to its occasional role in unfortunate hook-ups, hangovers, arrests, and…. how do I put this delicately…. unexpected surprises nine months later. For example, Founding Father Ben Franklin is often misquoted as saying, "Beer is living proof that God loves us and wants to see us happy." The scandalous truth behind the music here is that it was *wine* he was talking about, not beer. But who's to say we can't privately slip "beer" in there anyway and take the message to heart? However, Franklin did say, "There can't be good living where there is not good drinking." Beer lovers can certainly draw inspiration from that credo.

Even more shocking, a cover-up of biblical proportions has been alleged by many a beer scholar. It is believed that at the famed wedding feast at Canaan, Jesus actually turned the water into beer, not wine.

Beer has weathered the test of time to earn its five star accolades on the global stage. It is inextricably woven into the tapestry of our human existence. In doing so, it has repeatedly affirmed the famous folk lyric "In Heaven there is no beer…that's why we drink it here."

BEER'S WORLD TOUR THROUGH HISTORY

Like any tried and true rock star, beer has a *past*. Some put its age at 6,000 years, some at 7,000, others say it's even older, but this sudsy tease isn't talking, preferring some things be left to the imagination. What is known is that this illustrious icon started its journey in primitive villages and ancient civilizations through near simultaneous births at the far reaches of the world.

Sumerian women were the first people to brew beer. Mesopotamians sipped beer together through reed straws from a single bowl. Babylonians wrote beer recipes on clay tablets. Chinese villagers discovered the joys of individually brewing their favorite new beverage with millet and using it in religious rituals. In Egypt, the pharaohs had "royal chief beer inspectors" to insure the beverage's quality, the pyramid builders were paid with beer, and the dead were buried with *one for the road*, to the afterlife that is. And, Noah was even said to have served beer on the Ark. What a way to ride out a Great Flood!

Cherished Old World texts tell of beer's near mythical status as an elixir for prince and pauper alike. One of mankind's earliest known literary works, the *Epic of Gilgamesh* from Babylonia, extols the virtues of beer. As King Gilgamesh's friend, Enkidu, puts away several pitchers of the local brew, much like many a reveler might today, the author notes, "his heart grew light, his face glowed and he sang out with joy."

The Greek historian Xenophon recorded, "For drink, there was beer which was very strong when not mingled with water, but was agreeable to those who were used to it. They drank this with a reed, out of the vessel that held the beer, upon which they saw the barley swim."

The Egyptian *Book of the Dead* speaks of beer, relating it to such qualities as truth and eternity. Another popular ancient Egyptian saying held that "the mouth of a perfectly happy man is filled with beer."

Even the *Bible* recognizes the godly attributes of a good brew in Proverbs 31: 6-7: "Give beer to those who are perishing.... let them drink and forget their poverty and remember their misery no more." In Isaiah 56: 12, it is also written, "'Come,' each one cries, '...Let us drink our fill of beer! And tomorrow will be like today, or even far better.'"

The art of spinning this liquid gold in ancient times traveled through Greece, where Plato heralded, "He was a wise man who invented beer." From there, the secret to brewing was given to the Romans, who honored its chief ingredient, barley, on its coinage. Historians have long credited beer, along with bread, as the driving impetus behind the development of early technologies and civilization itself. One might then say, beer took us out of the caves and into the pubs of progress.

During the Middle Ages, creating and feasting on beer were favorite activities in the cottages, monasteries, and castles of Europe. Whether king or priest, laborer or barbarian, while weathering Crusades or societal evolution life was made easier by drinking beer. Often synonymous with beer, Bavaria, Germany, boasts the world's oldest commercial brewery still in operation, the Bayerische Staatsbrauerei Weihenstephan, dating back to 1040 when it was originally part of a Benedictine abbey.

Also hailing from Bavaria, beer made its early mark on the law when the Duke of Bavaria passed the cleanliness or purity law known as Reinheitsgebot on April 23, 1516. One of the world's oldest food regulations, the controversial Reinheitsgebot stated the creation of beer should be limited to water, barley, hops, and eventually yeast. The Reinheitsgebot also established the price of beer at 1 Pfennig (an old German coin) per measure (approximately 1 liter). Earlier still in the annuls of law, an 11th Century edict in the Polish northern city of Danzig stated, "Who-ever makes a poor beer is tranferred to the dung hill."

Of course, beer and its boozy buddies had their most headline-worthy brush with the law centuries later during Prohibition in the United States. Brewing was halted by the 18th Amendment to the U.S. Constitution, which prohibited the "manufacture, sale, or transportation of intoxicating liquors" and their importation and exportation. The Amendment was ratified by the necessary number of states on January 29, 1919.

At this time, many thought beer's low alcohol content would exempt it from this amendment, believing that "intoxicating liquors" referred only to such high alcohol beverages as whiskey, rum, and other distilled spirits. However, an ultra-religious congressman from Minnesota named Andrew J. Volstead defined "intoxicating liquors" as any beverage containing more than one half of one percent alcohol. Volstead's position prevailed in Congress and despite President Wilson's veto the period known as Prohibition went into effect on January 29, 1920. Because of Congressman Volstead's advocacy concerning this issue, the 18th Amendment is also called The Volstead Act.

During this time, many breweries relied on making near beer, a nonalcoholic take on the original, while other breweries were forced out of business. Of course, what would a golden rock star be without a few skeletons in the closet? More than a few rebellious brew masters out there continued to mine the alcohol-infused brew in all its glory, and covertly distributed it to devotees on the sly.

It was only a matter of time though before beer would once more have its day in the sun. Fourteen years later on December 5, 1933, the highly failed tenants of the 18th Amendment were officially repealed when Utah, Ohio, and Pennsylvania ratified the 21st Amendment, the only amendment to ever be adopted to repeal a prior amendment. Beer enjoyed a resounding comeback in the states as brewing once again officially commenced. Beer lovers everywhere lobbed a collective sigh of relief. Among them, President Franklin D. Roosevelt, who announced, "I believe this would be a good time for a beer."

Speaking of relief, throughout the ages, beer has also been praised for its supposed medicinal value, challenging that of its main rival, wine. Sumerians washed wounds with hot water and beer. Ancient Egyptian physicians had about a hundred medical prescriptions calling for beer and used beer to treat gum-disease. Anthropologists from Emory University discovered that the bones of ancient Nubians from along the Nile River contained tetracycline, an antibiotic that was produced as a result of the beer they consumed. And, the famous 16th century Swiss physician Paracelsus declared, "A little bit of beer is divine medicine."

In 1942, *The Carbon Copy* summarized, beer "is more to many drinkers in that it may be considered a specific against many of the ills of the body and mind. It is first a refresher and then a mild stimulant which wipes the cobwebs from dusty minds; it tones up the system, restores circulation, clears the eyes, and brings the rose back to faded cheeks."

Modern day research has lent credibility to this theory. Numerous studies have shown that the vitamins in most beer, such as antioxidants and the B vitamins niacin, riboflavin, B6, and folate, the soluble fiber, protein, and the other natural ingredients could be good for the heart. One such study yielding these results was conducted by the Beth Israel Deaconess Medical Center and the Harvard School of Public Health and reported in the *Archives of Internal Medicine*. Furthermore, beer's high potassium and low sodium content may help maintain a healthy blood pressure while a brewski or two could possibly help protect moderate drinkers against ulcers, stroke, hypertension, diabetes, some cancers, and other conditions.

To the delight of *avid* beer drinkers, researchers from the University College London and the Institute of Clinical and Experimental Medicine in Prague discovered that the term "beer belly" is incorrect. In the *European Journal of Clinical Nutrition*, they revealed how one's expansive waistline is not caused by beer, but by other factors. In addition, for the ladies who love their brew, the study also showed that women who drink beer actually weigh less than women who refrain. A study conducted by the University of Naples showed similar results, pointing the finger of blame for beer bellies at poor diet and lack of exercise.

Results from other studies on beer's link to good health have also been widely reported in such prestigious medical journals as *The Journal of the American Medical Association*, *The New England Journal of Medicine*, and the *British Medical Journal*. A study published in *The American Journal of Psychiatry* even heralded the benefits of "beer sociotherapy" in geriatric mental patients.

Finally, consider this: the late Hermann Doernemann of Germany, who died at age 111 years, 279 days, in 2005, credited his trek to becoming the second oldest man on the planet at the time to enjoying a beer each day. Just maybe then, like apples, a beer a day also keeps the doctor away. So drink to your good health…in moderation, of course.

On the monumental voyage of the Mayflower in 1620, beer helped sustain the pilgrims in mind, body, and spirit as they traveled across the Atlantic Ocean. More significantly, beer was one of the reasons the pilgrims unexpectedly landed on Plymouth Rock. Mayflower passenger and longtime Governor of Plymouth Colony, William Bradford, wrote of the trip in his historic journal, *Of Plymouth Plantation*: "We could not now take time for further search… our victuals being much spent, especially our beer…" Earlier still in the Americas, when Christopher Columbus first landed, he discovered Indians making beer from maize.

During the industrialization of the modern world beginning in the 1700s, beer traveled more freely without boundaries, reaching new audiences. By this time, it had become a cultural phenomenon the likes the world had never seen. Advancements with the steam engine and the invention of such technologies as the thermometer and hydrometer (for determining the gravity of liquids), and later the drum roaster (for dark, roasted malts), catapulted brew masters into a new era of brewing. Also, Louis Pasteur's research and experiments with yeast and fermentation further helped preserve and protect the taste integrity of beer.

From this era as well, the Declaration of Independence owes at least part of its origination to beer. Our forefathers, including Patrick Henry, Thomas Jefferson, Samuel Adams, and James Madison, were rousing advocates of beer and its potential to help define the new country's culture and commerce. Jefferson, who had his own private brew house, crafted large portions of the Declaration of Independence at the Indian Queen Tavern in Philadelphia, presumably over a few chilled brewskis. As president, he would quip, "Beer, if drank with moderation, softens the temper, cheers the spirit, and promotes health."

Beer has earned the presidential stamp of approval again and again. Our first President, George Washington, understood its power. He had his own brewery at Mount Vernon, one of the largest distilleries in the country at the time. He was the first of a long procession of American presidents who enjoyed a nip of brew. Lincoln once said, "I am a firm believer in the people. If given the truth, they can be depended upon to meet any national crisis. The great point is to bring them the real facts, and beer." Years later, Teddy Roosevelt took stashes of beer with him on African safaris. During his tenure, President Eisenhower once observed, "Some people wanted champagne and caviar when they should have had beer and hotdogs." In 1979, President Jimmy Carter signed a bill into law legalizing homebrewing, which ignited the art form and the ensuing legions of beer hobbyists.

Of course, there's then one of beer's biggest modern-day fans, a Founding Father in his own right, Homer J. Simpson. He sums up the sheer delight each sip of brew imparts upon beer lovers every time he utters, "Mmmmmm, beer." He also reworked a *Sound of Music* classic into a foamy tribute called "Doe Re

Mi Beer." This brew-toned Springfield native has further helped our golden rock star blaze its way into the utmost echelons of Pop Culture stardom.

Although during the earliest days of the American colonies the ales of England and the Netherlands became one of the most popular transplants to our shores, eventually with the influx of German immigrants also came their newly invented lagers.

It's at this benchmark in the genealogy of beer that my own family's story begins. It is a 19th century German immigrant, and his fellowship of brew masters, who is owed due credit for sparking this cookbook well over a century later.

THE MIDAS TOUCH

In 1869 at age nineteen, with only a few gold pieces sewn into his jacket, my Great-Great-Grandfather Peter Straub left his family in Felldorf, Wuerttemberg, Germany in search of the American Dream. With a last name whose origins date back to 530 B.C. in what would become Straubing, Germany, young Peter left everything that was familiar to him – the security of his parents, brothers, sisters, relatives, friends, his home. He had an immigrant's drive within him to pursue a better life, a more fulfilled life. This is undaunted humanity at its best, and a story that has been repeated in every family in one form or another.

Peter also carried one other thing with him on that long journey across the raging seas, something he would rework, refine, and develop into 100% gold: A recipe for beer. Little did he know at the time, but like beer's burgeoning kingmakers and his fellow countrymen of the same era—Milwaukee's Frederick Best and Frederick Pabst, founders of the Pabst Brewing Company started in 1844, Frederick Miller, who founded the Miller Brewing Company in 1855, and Joseph Schlitz, who created the Joseph Schlitz Brewing Company in 1856; Detroit's Bernhard Stroh, who opened Stroh Brewery in 1850; Golden, Colorado's Adolph Herman Joseph Coors, Sr., who founded Coors in 1873; St. Louis' Eberhard Anheuser and Adolphus Busch, who's Anheuser-Busch Company was launched in 1852, and Louis Koch, whose 1860 beer recipe launched the Samuel Adams brand in 1985; and Pottsville, Pennsylvania's David G. Yuengling, who started D.G. Yuengling & Son in 1829—Peter, too, possessed the Midas Touch.

As one local writer stated of this pivotal time: "Up to 1840, 'British' type of beer dominated the American scene, but enough is enough, the Germans said and took it upon themselves to educate the Americans on real beer, the lager variety, which is today America's basic taste bud wetter."

Upon arriving in his new homeland, Peter settled in Allegheny City, PA, working at the Eberhardt and Ober Brewing Company. There he enlisted his skills as a cooper, which is a craftsman trained in making and repairing wooden barrels and casks. He had honed these talents in his native Germany, as well as in France and Switzerland. Peter next moved to Brookville where he worked at the Christ and Allgeier Brewery.

In 1872, Peter finally put down roots in the small German settlement of St. Marys, PA, which boasted numerous breweries at the time. However, this is where he would outlast all the others, giving birth to a local legend and, in doing so, help contribute to beer's international acclaim.

After arriving in the town he would call home for the rest of his life, my great-great-grandfather first worked at the Windfelder Brewery. With fate and faith ever at his side, Peter eventually went to work for his future father-in-law's brewery. He worked his way up through the company, to become the brew master. He also met and fell in love with the boss' daughter, my great-great-grandmother, Sabina.

By 1878, Peter's dream became a reality: He bought his father-in-law's brewery, becoming the company president. He now had his slice of the American pie.

Today, my great-great-grandfather's brewery, like those of his fellow 19th Century brewing alumni, has spanned three different centuries and the threshold of a new millennium. Peter's brewery also bears the distinction of being one of the oldest breweries in the country to still be owned and operated by its founding family, now into its sixth generation.

The Straub Brewery has remained a small macrobrewery, as well as a craft brewery, where most of the work is orchestrated by human hands and not delegated to elaborate machinery for mass production. Aside from its award-winning brew, my great-great-grandfather's brewery has contributed an iconic marker of its own to the history of beer, one that has drawn beer fans from around the world: The Eternal Tap.

The most popular site at the brewery, The Eternal Tap is located just outside of the production area. Installed decades ago, visitors are invited to enjoy a complimentary taste of the house specialty. Originally, the beer was served in tin cups. Today, the tin cups have been replaced with glass mugs as Straub Beer continues to perpetually flow and satisfy visitors.

Bob Batz, Jr. of *The Pittsburgh Press Sunday Magazine*, introduced The Eternal Tap to the masses: "Another legend has to do with another kind of locally prized gold—beer—that is said to flow freely and forever, a la the Fountain of Youth, from something called 'the Eternal Tap.' Thirsty souls seek the tap near the center of St. Marys, and usually find it. The Eternal Tap is real." An Associated Press article also sent news of the attraction around the country, garnering stories in newspapers as far away as Hawaii, Florida, and Canada.

During the early 1980s, my great-great-grandfather's brewery almost scored a lead role in the movie *Take This Job and Shove It*, based on the popular Johnny Paycheck song. Unfortunately, in the end, the role went to a *much younger* brewery from Iowa.

For me, this tale of a young man who sought and grabbed hold of his destiny, and whose blood I share, has inspired me. I'm not skilled in ways that would make me beneficial on the production floor of his brewery today, but I've realized that my gift is as a writer. It has been in this way then that I have chosen to honor and promote Peter's tasty legacy...and the almighty BEER.

WHERE THE GOLD FLOWS

The first-recorded recipe for beer is 3,900 years old and is of mythical proportions. "The Hymn of Ninkasi," originally found etched into a stone tablet, is devoted to the Sumerian goddess of brewing. She shares this billing with Siris, also a Mesopotamian goddess of brewers. Likewise, the traditional Greek and Roman wine-god, Dionysus, is said to have started out as the god of beer, but the debate rages on about that one.

The stanzas pertinent to Ninkasi's beer recipe are as follows, translated by Sumerology Professor Miguel Civil:

You are the one who soaks the malt in a jar,
The waves rise, the waves fall.
Ninkasi, you are the one who soaks the malt in a jar,
The waves rise, the waves fall.

You are the one who spreads the cooked mash on large reed mats,
Coolness overcomes....
Ninkasi, you are the one who spreads the cooked mash on large reed mats,
Coolness overcomes....

You are the one who holds with both hands the great sweetwort,
Brewing (it) with honey (and) wine.
Ninkasi, you are the one who holds with both hands the great sweetwort,
Brewing (it) with honey (and) wine.

[...]
[You...the sweetwort to the vessel].
Ninkasi, [...],
[You...] the sweetwort to the vessel.

The fermenting vat, which makes a pleasant sound,
You place appropriately on (top of) a large collector vat.
Ninkasi, the fermenting vat, which makes a pleasant sound,
You place appropriately on (top of) a large collector vat.

You are the one who pours out the filtered beer of the collector vat,
It is (like) the onrush of the Tigris and the Euphrates.
Ninkasi, you are the one who pours out the filtered beer of the collector vat,
It is (like) the onrush of the Tigris and the Euphrates.

Ninkasi, you are the one who pours out the filtered beer of the collector vat,
It is [like] the onrush of Tigris and Euphrates.

Of all the many gods and goddesses of beer throughout the different cultures, Ninkasi's main competition may be Mbaba Mwana Waresa, the beloved South African Zulu Goddess of Beer. Many believe she was the first to invent beer for us mere mortals to savor.

Throughout the millennia of beer production and consumption, the recipes have changed, evolved, and progressed into the 21st century, especially concerning technologies and advancements in the art of crafting beer.

Although every brew master and homebrew crafter applies his or her own secrets to polishing their unique brand of gold, I'm going to take you inside a brewing process that has remained relatively unchanged for more than 130 years. This is from a small brewery with an output of about 48,000 bottles and 145 barrels of beer during each day of production. Consider this a rare behind-the-scenes glimpse at our favorite golden rock star in private.

The beer recipe begins at 4 A.M. with its main ingredient, mountain-fed spring and stream water. 5,000 gallons of water are used during one day of brewing. The water is combined with cornflakes and crushed malted barley and mixed in the Mash-Lauter Tun or Mash Tub.

The starch from the grains is converted into fermentable sugar by the natural enzymes contained in the malted barley. The mixing process lasts for 2½ hours at temperatures ranging from 104° to 170°, producing a sweet golden syrup called wort.

The wort is slowly drawn through a copper vessel called a Grant where it is visually inspected for the two highly coveted C's of brewing, clarity and color, much like with diamonds.
Next, hops extract is added as the wort is transferred through the Grant to the Brew Kettle where it is boiled for 2 hours. A Percolator ensures a rolling boil so as to super heat the bottom of the kettle and send the heat upwards throughout the kettle during the brewing process.

The heated mixture is then held in a separate vessel for a short time before being cooled to approximately 54° as it passes through an enclosed Wort Cooling System at a rate of one barrel per minute. It then proceeds to the Fermenting Tanks.

The fermenting process begins with the addition of liquid yeast to the unfermented beer. The fermenting process takes seven days, during which time the yeast will consume the fermentable sugars in the wort, producing beer and, as a byproduct, carbon dioxide, which is collected and filtered.

After the fermentation process is completed, the beer is transferred to a 38° cellar for aging and double filtering.

During primary filtration, which is called roughing, and secondary filtration, which is called polishing, the filtered carbon dioxide is injected into the beer.

The beer is then transferred to either the Racking Room, where it is hand-racked or placed into kegs, or to the Bottling House.

Finally, the beer is ready to end up in the hands of thirsty beer lovers everywhere. Or how about in your pizza sauce or juicy pork roast?

Having endured the trends and fads of history, and a medieval war or two, one thing is certain about beer: With it, anything is possible.

HAVE YOUR BEER, AND EAT IT TOO!

My earliest memory of food made with beer is as a child eating my mother's holiday ham. She still makes it by inserting twenty cloves into a five pound ham, placing it in a roaster, pouring a bottle of beer over top, and baking it for three hours. My mouth waters just thinking about it.

Imagine if you could start your day with beer and end it with beer, and *not* have a headache the next morning. Then, imagine your favorite foods—dips, breads, creamy soups, vegetables, steaks, burgers, pizza, wings, seafood, ice cream, and even desserts—all infused with beer. From dawn until dusk, and beyond, *The Ultimate Beer Lover's Cookbook* is your indulgent, finishing guide to becoming the *ultimate* beer connoisseur.

Now, picture the perfect day, whether you live in the frenzy of the city, the down-home charm of the country, or somewhere in between. A hearty plate of scrambled eggs made with beer and beer bread toast topped with herbed beer butter for breakfast. A dandelion salad, seafood gumbo, or cheese steak sandwich with a side order of onion rings, all made with beer for lunch. Or, perhaps you'd prefer a traditional beer burger and chocolate beershake at noon.

An afternoon indulgence of chocolate-dipped strawberries and bananas, again made with beer. And, an early dinner of drunken chicken, garlic roast beef, or perhaps a surf 'n' turf beer combo of lobster and marinated & stuffed flank steak, with a slice of golden beer cheesecake for dessert.

Later on that evening, you'll be *the* host with the most as you dazzle your guests with a selection of wings in blazing hot sauce, crab dip, salsa, honey mustard, deviled eggs, stuffed tomatoes, shrimp with cocktail sauce, calamari, apple rings, cinnamon & walnut cookies, fried ice cream balls, and a selection of mixed drinks, chuggers, shots & shooters, chasers, punches, and perhaps a vanilla cream float to wash it all down with—*all made with beer.*

And, don't forget that midnight snack after the guests all leave. A thick slice of beer pizza and a few of those left over chocolate-dipped strawberries and bananas from earlier in the day.

This is perfection you can taste all day long!

From the old world to the modern global village, cooks have always used beer as a cooking ingredient. A favorite brewski adds zest and enhanced flavor to almost any dish. The best part is that there are very few rules you have to follow. Even the most novice chefs out there can turn their meals and parties into celebratory brew fests.

Because it works in mysterious ways with different foods, it's hard to adequately describe the magic beer adds to food, other then to say there's an obvious void when it's not there. To leave beer out of food is to torment the pallet *and* the psyche, a neglect akin to committing a culinary crime.

When talking about beer recipes, and particularly this collection, I always impart one rule of thumb to my audience: Trust your own taste buds. I like to think of the more than 400 recipes in this book as works-in-progress, much like any collection of recipes. No recipe is ever truly complete until each individual person holding the whisk or the spatula or, most importantly in this case, the measuring cup adds his or her very own pinch of this or dash of that. If you want a little less beer in your glazed carrots or chicken with shiitake mushrooms, or if you want to punch up your sweet 'n' tangy pork sauté and twin fudge cakes with more beer, go for it.

Although the recipes herein work well with a good classic lager, I hope you'll experiment with the endless line-up of specialty beers on the market today. Perhaps you have your own homebrew you can add to the mix, truly making these recipes homegrown superstars.

Remember, you're the host with the most of this ultimate beer lover's party. You make the rules.

Also, like any multi-talented rock star, beer has had many famous collaborations on the bar circuit. It has teamed-up with other such greats as gin, vodka, whiskey, tequila, and, yes, even wine!

From the Buzzy Navel, Beer Bullet, Red-Headed Mary, and Beertini to the Woodpecker, Strawberry Jolt, Atomic Diva, Wild Turkey Chase, Garden of Eden Punch, and Flaming Sake Bomb, this anthology of beer's greatest pairings is sure to leave you spinning for joy. A Triple Mint Float never tasted better, a Root Beer Float never had such pizzazz, and for a true crowd pleaser, trust me, you'll never disappoint when you serve up a Tongue Tingler or Skip & Go Naked.

The Ultimate Beer Lover's Cookbook lives up to its title in delivering a high quality and unprecedented quantity of beer-inspired choices. Consider this your bible of beer, where even gluttony becomes a tempting virtue. This is your loyal kitchen companion, and your secret weapon to throwing the ultimate bash, whether it be for a few friends, a few dozen guests, or just you.

BEER = FUN!

Adopt this motto and with this book to guide you, you've got your very own VIP pass into the sudsy revelry of the world's most celebrated, hopheaded rock star.

The Ultimate

Beer Lover's

Cookbook

CHAPTER 1

Appetizers

❖⦃ LEEK SPREAD ⦄❖

· Yields 5½ Cups

1	pound sharp Cheddar cheese, shredded
1	pound mild Cheddar cheese, shredded
3	tablespoons ketchup
1	tablespoon Dijon mustard
1	tablespoon Worcestershire sauce
1	leek or 2 scallions, trimmed and minced, white part only
1	clove garlic, peeled and minced
¼	teaspoon hot red pepper sauce
1½	to 2 cups flat beer

In an electric mixer at high speed or in a food processor fitted with a metal chopping blade, blend all of the ingredients, except the beer, until the mixture is smooth.

With the motor running, pour the beer into the mixture in a slow steady stream until the mixture is as thick as you prefer. Pack the Leek Spread into a storage container, cover, and refrigerate for several days to mellow the flavors.

"YOU SIT BACK IN THE DARKNESS, NURSING YOUR BEER, BREATHING IN THAT INEFFABLE AROMA OF THE OLD-TIME SALOON: DARK WOOD, SPILLED BEER, GOOD CIGARS, AND ANCIENT WHISKEY—THE SACRED INCENSE OF THE DRINKING MAN."

Bruce Aidells, American chef

❧ CLASSIC DIP ☙

· Yields 3 Cups

1	8-ounce package cream cheese
1	5-ounce jar Old English sharp cheese spread
1	teaspoon parsley
	Garlic salt to taste
½	cup light beer

In a bowl, combine all of the ingredients except the light beer until the mixture is smooth. Then while continuing to mix, pour the light beer into the mixture until it is as thick as you prefer. For the best taste, pack the Classic Dip into a storage container, cover, and refrigerate overnight, allowing the flavors to settle.

❧ BLACK BEAN DIP ☙

· Yields 3½ Cups

1	8-ounce package cream cheese, softened
8	ounces Cheddar cheese with jalapeño peppers, cubed
⅓	cup beer
1	cup black beans, drained and rinsed
½	cup sliced scallions
½	cup chopped tomatoes
	Tortilla chips

In a medium saucepan over low heat, combine the cream cheese, Cheddar cheese, and beer, mixing well until the cheeses are melted. Add the black beans, scallions, and tomatoes, mixing well. Serve the Black Bean Dip warm with the tortilla chips.

❧ CRAB DIP ❧

· Yields 3 Cups

1½	cups mayonnaise
1	teaspoon mustard
¼	teaspoon hot pepper sauce
	Dash of lemon juice
	Seasoned salt to taste
2	tablespoons beer
6	ounces Alaskan crab meat, separated

In a bowl, combine the mayonnaise, mustard, pepper sauce, lemon juice, seasoned salt, and beer. Mix until smooth. Stir in the crab meat.

❧ CRAB BOWL DIP ❧

· Yields 10 to 12 Servings

12	ounces crab meat
2	8-ounce packages cream cheese, softened
2	tablespoons beer
1	teaspoon lemon juice
½	teaspoon Worcestershire sauce
	Dash of hot sauce
¼	teaspoon salt (or to taste)
	Round loaf of rye bread or crackers of choice

In a large bowl, combine all of the ingredients, except the rye bread, mixing well. Add extra seasonings to taste. Slice the top off the rye bread and scoop out the center. Place the beer crab mixture into the rye bread bowl. Serve with the scooped-out rye bread chunks or crackers.

❧ BLUE CHEESE DIP ❧

· Yields 2 Cups

3	6-ounce rolls sharp cheese, softened
1½	ounces blue cheese (Roquefort)
2	tablespoons butter, softened
2	medium cloves garlic, minced
1	medium onion
1	teaspoon Worcestershire sauce
½	teaspoon Tabasco sauce
1	cup beer (warm)
1	loaf rye bread or crackers of choice

In a large bowl, combine all of the ingredients except the beer and rye bread, mixing well with an electric mixer. Slowly add the beer, continuing to mix well. Refrigerate the mixture. Serve the Blue Cheese Dip cold with the rye bread or crackers.

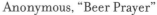

"Our lager,
Which art in barrels,
Hallowed be thy drink.
Thy will be drunk, (I will be drunk), At home as it is in the pub.
Give us this day our foamy head,
And forgive us our spillages,
As we forgive those who spill against us.
And lead us not to incarceration, But deliver us from hangovers.
For thine is the beer, The bitter, The lager.
Forever and ever,
Barmen."

Anonymous, "Beer Prayer"

❊{ FONDUE }❊

· Yields 4 to 6 Servings

1	small clove garlic, halved
3/4	cup beer
2	cups shredded Swiss cheese
1	cup shredded sharp natural Cheddar cheese
1	tablespoon all-purpose flour
	Dash of hot pepper sauce
	Dippers of choice (examples: chicken, steak, raw vegetables)

Use the cut side of the garlic to coat the inside of a saucepan and then discard the garlic. Pour the beer into the saucepan and heat it slowly. On a cutting board, coat the shredded cheeses with the flour. Gradually add the cheese to the beer, stirring constantly, until the mixture is thickened and bubbles. Do not allow the mixture to become too hot. Stir in the hot pepper sauce. Transfer the mixture to a fondue pot. Place the pot over the fondue burner.

Spear each dipper with a fondue fork, dipping it into the fondue, swirling to coat. If the mixture becomes too thick, stir in a little additional warmed beer.

"HE WHO DRINKS BEER SLEEPS WELL.
HE WHO SLEEPS WELL CANNOT SIN.
HE WHO DOES NOT SIN GOES TO HEAVEN.
AMEN."

Unknown German Monk

❖{ MEATBALLS }❖

· Yields 32 Meatballs

2	slices bread, cubed
12	ounces beer
1	pound lean ground beef
½	cup shredded mozzarella cheese
	Freshly ground black pepper to taste
½	cup chopped onion
1	tablespoon butter
2	tablespoons brown sugar
2	tablespoons vinegar
2	tablespoons beef stock
1	to 2 tablespoons all-purpose flour (optional)
	Sauce of choice

In one bowl, soak the bread cubes in ½ cup of beer. In another bowl, combine the ground beef, mozzarella cheese, pepper, and beer-soaked bread. Shape the mixture into 32 cocktail-size meatballs. Arrange the meatballs in a single layer on a cookie sheet and bake for 15 minutes at 350°. When the meatballs are done, drain them on paper towels to remove the grease.

In a skillet, sauté the onions in butter until tender. Stir in the brown sugar, vinegar, beef stock, and remaining beer. Thicken with flour if desired. Simmer the mixture over a low heat for 10 minutes. Add the meatballs to the sauce and simmer for 20 minutes.

"ALWAYS REMEMBER THAT I HAVE TAKEN MORE OUT OF ALCOHOL THAN ALCOHOL HAS TAKEN OUT OF ME."

Winston Churchill, British Prime Minister

❋❴ STEAMED SAUSAGE ❵❋

· Yields 8 to 10 Servings

12	ounces beer
	Smoked sausage (enough to fill a crock-pot), cut into bite-size pieces

Pour the beer into the bottom of a crock-pot. Add the smoked sausage pieces. Cook the sausage on high for 2 hours. Switch to low until it is time to serve the sausage.

❋❴ SAUSAGE BITES ❵❋

· Yields 6 to 8 Servings

2	pounds smoked sausage, cooked and cut into ½-inch slices
1	cup beer
¼	cup brown sugar
2	tablespoons cornstarch
¼	cup vinegar
1	tablespoon horseradish
¼	cup mustard

In a skillet, combine the sausage and beer, cover, and simmer the mixture for 10 minutes.

In a small bowl, combine the brown sugar and cornstarch, mixing well. Stir in the vinegar, horseradish, and mustard, mixing well. Add this mixture to the sausage mixture, cooking and stirring until it is bubbly.

⁂{ CHEESE BITES }⁂

· Yields 80 Bites

2	cups Bisquick baking mix
½	cup shredded Cheddar cheese
½	cup beer
2	tablespoons butter, melted
	Sesame seeds

Preheat the oven to 450°. In a large bowl, combine the baking mix, Cheddar cheese, and beer, mixing well and then beating well for approximately 15 to 20 strokes.

On a floured board, form the dough into a ball and then knead it 5 times. Roll the dough out into a rectangle approximately 16 x 10-inches. Cut the dough into 2-inch squares and then cut each of those squares diagonally in half. Spread the butter over the halves and sprinkle them with the sesame seeds. Place the halves on ungreased cookie sheets. Bake the Cheese Bites for about 7 to 8 minutes or until they are browned.

"GIVE BEER TO THOSE WHO ARE PERISHING, WINE TO THOSE WHO ARE IN ANGUISH; LET THEM DRINK AND FORGET THEIR POVERTY AND REMEMBER THEIR MISERY NO MORE."

Bible (Proverbs 31:6-7)

❈{ CHEDDAR CHEESE SPREAD }❈

· Yields 4 to 6 Servings

1	pound Cheddar cheese, grated
½	large clove garlic, minced (or to taste)
½	tablespoon Worcestershire sauce
½	tablespoon dry mustard
½	teaspoon salt
½	cup beer

In a blender or food processor, combine all of the ingredients, except the beer. When well blended, gradually add all of the beer, continuing to blend. Place the Cheddar Cheese Spread into a storage container, cover, and refrigerate for at least 24 hours.

"KEEP YOUR LIBRARIES, YOUR PENAL INSTI-
TUTIONS, YOUR INSANE ASYLUMS... GIVE ME
BEER. YOU THINK MAN NEEDS RULE, HE
NEEDS BEER. THE WORLD DOES NOT NEED
MORALS, IT NEEDS BEER... THE SOULS OF
MEN HAVE BEEN FED WITH INDIGESTIBLES,
BUT THE SOUL COULD MAKE USE OF BEER."

Henry Miller, American author

⁂{ SPICY CHEDDAR CHEESE SPREAD }⁂

· Yields 12 Servings

12	ounces flat beer
1½	pounds Cheddar cheese, cubed (room temperature)
2	tablespoons Worcestershire sauce
1	clove garlic, minced (or to taste)
3	to 4 drops hot pepper sauce
	Salt and pepper to taste (optional)

Pour the beer into a blender or food processor. Put the Cheddar cheese into the blender with the beer. Add the Worcestershire sauce, garlic, and hot pepper sauce. Blend the ingredients to a coarse purée. Season the mixture with salt and pepper to taste. Pack the Spicy Cheddar Cheese Spread into a storage container, cover, and refrigerate for at least 8 hours to blend the flavors.

"Sometimes when I reflect back on all the beer I drink I feel ashamed. Then I look into the glass and think about the workers in the brewery and all of their hopes and dreams. If I didn't drink this beer, they might be out of work and their dreams would be shattered. Then I say to myself, It is better that I drink this beer and let their dreams come true than be selfish and worry about my liver."

Jack Handey, American humorist

❧ SHARP CHEDDAR CHEESE CRACKERS ❧

· Yields 16 Crackers

¼	cup + 2 teaspoons all-purpose flour
¼	teaspoon double-acting baking powder
	Dash of salt
2	teaspoons butter
¼	cup beer
1	ounce sharp Cheddar cheese, shredded
½	teaspoon poppy seed

Preheat the oven to 450°. In a bowl, combine the flour, baking powder, and salt. Cut in the butter until the mixture resembles coarse meal. Add the beer and Cheddar cheese and stir the mixture to combine. Drop the batter in individual heaping teaspoonfuls onto a nonstick baking sheet. Form 16 mounds leaving 1-inch between each. Sprinkle each mound with an equal amount of poppy seed. Bake for about 8 to 10 minutes until lightly browned. Remove the crackers to a wire rack to cool.

"NOT ALL CHEMICALS ARE BAD. WITHOUT CHEMICALS SUCH AS HYDROGEN AND OXYGEN, FOR EXAMPLE, THERE WOULD BE NO WAY TO MAKE WATER, A VITAL INGREDIENT IN BEER."

Dave Barry, American humorist

⊰ DEVILED EGGS ⊱

· Yields 12 Deviled Eggs

6	eggs, hard-boiled, peeled, halved, and separated
1	teaspoon vinegar
1	tablespoon mayonnaise
½	teaspoon Worcestershire sauce
¼	teaspoon salt
	Pepper to taste
¾	teaspoon mustard
1	teaspoon to 1 tablespoon beer (depending on preference)
12	olives

In a bowl, combine the egg yolks and remaining ingredients except the olives. With a small spoon, scoop the mixture into the egg halves. Garnish each Deviled Egg with an olive.

"THERE IS AN ANCIENT CELTIC AXIOM THAT SAYS 'GOOD PEOPLE DRINK GOOD BEER.' WHICH IS TRUE, THEN AS NOW. JUST LOOK AROUND YOU IN ANY PUBLIC BARROOM AND YOU WILL QUICKLY SEE: BAD PEOPLE DRINK BAD BEER. THINK ABOUT IT."

Hunter S. Thompson, American journalist and author

❧ STUFFED TOMATOES ❧

• Yields 8 to 12 Servings

8	large or 10 to 12 medium tomatoes
	Salt and pepper to taste
	Seasoned salt to taste
12	ounces whole corn, drained
1	small onion, finely chopped
1	small to medium sized green pepper, finely chopped
8	ounces sharp Cheddar cheese, grated
3	cups soft bread crumbs
2	cups beer
	Ranch dressing (if desired)

Cut the tops off the tomatoes and remove the pulp. Season the inside of the tomatoes with the salt, pepper, and seasoned salt to taste.

In a large bowl, combine all of the other ingredients, mixing well. Scoop the ingredients into the hollow tomatoes. Pour or brush more beer onto the tops of the stuffed tomatoes. Bake the tomatoes in a hot oven for 15 to 20 minutes. Serve with Ranch dressing on the side, if desired.

"'COME,' EACH ONE CRIES, 'LET ME GET WINE! LET US DRINK OUR FILL OF BEER! AND TOMORROW WILL BE LIKE TODAY, OR EVEN FAR BETTER.'"

Bible (Isaiah 56: 12)

⁂{ CRAB BALLS }⁂

· Yields 30 Balls

1	cup beer
½	cup (1 stick) butter
1	cup sifted all-purpose flour
½	teaspoon seasoned salt
4	eggs
1	7-ounce can crab meat

In a saucepan, combine the beer and butter, mixing well. Bring the mixture to a boil. Add the flour and seasoned salt, mixing well. Beat in the eggs. On a greased baking sheet, drop tea-spoon-size amounts of the batter, making sure they are about 1 to 2-inches apart. Cover with foil. Bake the balls at 450° for approximately 8 to 10 minutes. Reduce the heat to 350° and bake the balls for 10 minutes until they are browned. After the balls cool, slice them open as desired and fill them with the crabmeat to serve.

"For every wound, a balm.
For every sorrow, cheer.
For every storm, a calm.
For every thirst, a beer."

Anonymous

❊{ SALSA }❊

· Yields 2 Cups

6	chile peppers
1	cup beer
1	clove garlic
	Juice from 1 orange
¼	medium onion, chopped
	Salt to taste
½	cup crumbled white cheese
	Tortilla chips

In a skillet, toast the chile peppers over a medium flame until they blister. Open the chile peppers and remove the stems, veins, and seeds. Soak the chile peppers in the beer for 30 minutes. In a blender, combine the chile peppers, beer, garlic, and orange juice, puréeing until the mixture is smooth. Stir in the onion and add the salt to taste. Garnish with the cheese and serve with the tortilla chips.

"Mother's in the kitchen washing out the jugs,
Sister's in the pantry bottling the suds,
Father's in the cellar mixin' up the hops,
Johnny's on the front porch watchin' for the cops."

Prohibition song

CHAPTER 2

Breads, Pancakes, & Doughs

❧ BASIL BREAD ❧

· Yields 1 Loaf

3	cups self-rising flour
3	tablespoons sugar
½	cup chopped fresh basil
½	cup beer (warm)

Preheat the oven to 350°. Grease a 9 x 5-inch loaf pan.

In a large bowl, combine the flour and sugar, mixing well. Stir in the basil, mixing well. Add the beer, mixing well. Pour the mixture into the prepared pan. Bake for about 50 minutes or until a toothpick inserted in the center comes out clean. Cool the Basil Bread on a wire rack.

❧ OAT & RYE BREAD ❧

· Yields 1 Loaf

1	package dry yeast
2¼	cups whole wheat flour
1¼	cups stale beer
1½	teaspoons salt
1½	tablespoons vegetable oil
1½	tablespoons oat flour
1½	cups rye flour

In a large bowl, combine all of the ingredients, mixing well. Place the mixture in an electric bread maker and process on the white bread cycle.

⋑ ORANGE RYE BREAD ⋐

· Yields 1 Loaf

1	package yeast
¼	cup warm water (to dissolve the yeast)
2	tablespoons applesauce
2	teaspoons grated orange peel
2	tablespoons molasses
1	cup beer
1	teaspoon salt
2	tablespoons wheat germ (crude)
2½	cups all-purpose flour (or more, if needed)
1	cup rye flour (medium)

Preheat the oven to 350°. Spray a loaf pan with cooking spray. Dissolve the yeast in the warm water. In a large bowl, combine all of the ingredients. Place the mixture in the prepared pan. Bake for 30 to 45 minutes or until a toothpick inserted in the center comes out clean. Cool the Orange Rye Bread on a wire rack.

"HERE'S TO A LONG LIFE, AND A MERRY ONE; A QUICK DEATH, AND AN EASY ONE; A PRETTY GIRL, AND AN HONEST ONE; A COLD BEER— AND ANOTHER ONE!"

Irish toast

❊{ PRETZEL BREAD }❊

· Yields 1 Loaf

1	package yeast
1/4	teaspoon ginger
1/4	teaspoon sugar
3	cups all-purpose flour
2	tablespoons gluten
1	teaspoon salt
1/8	teaspoon baking soda
1 1/3	cups thin pretzel stick halves
1	egg white
1	tablespoon vegetable oil
12	ounces beer
1/4	cup warm water

In a large bowl, combine all of the ingredients in the order listed, mixing well. Place the mixture in an electric bread maker and process on the white bread cycle.

"THE GOOD LORD HAS CHANGED WATER INTO WINE, SO HOW CAN DRINKING BEER BE A SIN?"

Sign near a Belgian Monastery

❧ ONION CHEESE BREAD ☙

· Yields 1 Loaf

3	cups all-purpose flour
1	tablespoon baking powder
3	tablespoons sugar
1	cup grated Cheddar cheese
4	scallions, chopped
1½	cups beer
1	egg, beaten
1	teaspoon sesame seeds

Preheat the oven to 350°. In a large bowl, combine the flour, baking powder, sugar, Cheddar cheese, and scallions, mixing well. Stir in the beer, mixing until the batter is sticky. Pour the batter into an 8½ x 4½-inch greased loaf pan. Brush the top of the loaf with the egg. Sprinkle the sesame seeds on top of the loaf. Bake the loaf for approximately 1¼ hours or until the loaf is browned. Cool the loaf on a wire rack.

Said, upon the ratification of the 21st Amendment repealing Prohibition:"I believe this would be a good time for a beer."
Franklin D. Roosevelt, 32nd U.S. President

❧ OLD-FASHIONED COUNTRY BREAD ❧

· Yields 2 Loaves

⅓	cup (5 tablespoons plus 1 teaspoon) butter
¾	cup milk
1	cup wheat germ
1½	cups beer
2	envelopes fast-acting yeast
2	tablespoons honey
⅓	cup molasses
6	cups whole wheat flour

In a skillet, combine and warm the butter and milk over a low heat. Add the wheat germ, stirring well. In another skillet, heat the beer until it is just below the boiling point. Add the yeast to the beer. After about 8 to 12 minutes as the beer mixture foams, add the cooled milk mixture. Stir in the honey, molasses, and whole wheat flour, mixing well until a sticky dough is formed. Remove the dough from the skillet and knead it on a floured board until it is smooth. Place the dough into a large greased bowl, rolling the dough to coat the surface. Cover the bowl with a floured towel. Put the dough in a warm place, allowing the dough to rise until it is twice its original size.

Turn the dough out onto a floured board and knead it for approximately 2 to 4 minutes. Divide the dough into 2 separate mounds and place each loaf into an 8½ x 4½-inch greased loaf pan. Cover each loaf pan and allow the loaves to double again to twice their original size.

Preheat the oven to 375°. Bake the loaves for 1 hour. Cool the loaves on a wire rack.

"HISTORY FLOWS FORWARD IN RIVERS OF BEER."

Anonymous

❧ MICROWAVABLE BREAD ❧

· Yields 1 Loaf

2	cups self-rising flour
1	cup all-purpose flour
3	tablespoons sugar
12	ounces beer
1	tablespoon butter, softened
	Cornflake crumbs

Completely coat the surface of a glass loaf pan with cooking spray.

In a large bowl, combine all of the ingredients except the cornflake crumbs, mixing well. Sprinkle the bottom and sides of the loaf pan with the cornflake crumbs. Pour the dough into the loaf pan. Microwave the dough on medium for 9 minutes and then on high for 2 minutes.

❧ GREEN CHILE CHEESE BREAD ❧

· Yields 1 Loaf

1	cup chopped green chile pepper
1	cup shredded Cheddar cheese
3	cups self-rising flour
3	tablespoons sugar
12	ounces beer

Preheat the oven to 350°. In a blender, combine the green chile pepper and Cheddar cheese, mixing well until the mixture is smooth. In a large bowl, combine the green chile pepper mixture, flour, sugar, and beer, mixing well until a sticky dough forms. Place the dough into a 9 x 5-inch greased loaf pan. Bake the loaf for approximately 1 hour or until the top is a golden brown. Cool the loaf on a wire rack.

❧ DRIED TOMATO BREAD ❧

· Yields 1 Loaf

¼	cup sugar
3½	cups self-rising flour
12	ounces beer
1	egg
¼	cup tomato sauce
2	ounces dried tomatoes

Preheat the oven to 350°. In a medium bowl, combine the sugar and flour, mixing well. Add the beer, egg, and tomato sauce, mixing well. Fold in the dried tomatoes. Place the dough into a greased loaf pan. Bake the dough for approximately 1 hour. Cool the loaf on a wire rack.

❧ SWEET BREAD ❧

· Yields 1 Loaf

3	cups self-rising flour
¾	cup firmly packed brown sugar
1	teaspoon ground cinnamon
12	ounces beer
½	cup raisins (optional)
½	cup chopped walnuts (optional)

In a bowl, combine all of the ingredients. Pour the mixture into a loaf pan. Bake at 350° for 45 minutes. Remove the bread and let it cool on a rack.

❧ EVERYDAY BREAD ❧

· Yields 2 Loaves

3	envelopes active dry yeast
½	cup lukewarm water
1½	cups beer (room temperature)
2	tablespoons sugar
2	teaspoons salt
1	egg, lightly beaten
½	cup whole wheat flour
5	cups unbleached flour
	Butter (for the bowl)
2	tablespoons milk

In an unbuttered bowl, dissolve the yeast in the lukewarm water and let the mixture rest for 5 minutes. Stir in the beer, sugar, salt, and egg. Add the whole wheat flour and 4 cups of the unbleached flour. Stir the mixture with a wooden spoon until it becomes a sticky dough. Turn the dough out onto a bread board and knead in the remaining 1 cup of unbleached flour, a little at a time, until the dough is smooth and elastic. Knead the dough for about 10 minutes more, until blisters form on the surface or until the dough springs back when touched. Place the dough into a buttered bowl, turn it to coat with butter, and cover it loosely with a cloth towel. Let the dough rise in a warm place for about 1 hour or until it is double in bulk.

Punch the dough down and divide it into 2 round loaves. Make 4 parallel slashes in the top of each loaf and let the dough rise in a warm place, covered loosely with towels, for 30 to 45 minutes.

Preheat the oven to 375°.

Brush the tops of the loaves with the milk and bake them for 30 minutes.

❧ LIGHT BEER BREAD ❧

· Yields 1 Loaf

1	cup whole wheat flour
1	cup all-purpose flour
½	cup old-fashioned rolled oats (Quaker Oats)
2	tablespoons sugar
2	teaspoons baking powder
½	teaspoon baking soda
½	teaspoon salt
1½	cups light beer (cold or at room temperature)

Position a rack in the lower third of the oven. Preheat the oven to 400°. In a bowl, thoroughly whisk together the whole wheat flour, all-purpose flour, rolled oats, sugar, baking powder, baking soda, and salt. Add the light beer and fold the mixture until the dry ingredients are moistened. Scrape the batter into a loaf pan and spread evenly. Bake the bread for about 35 to 40 minutes until a toothpick inserted in the center and all the way to the bottom of the pan comes out clean.

Let the bread cool in the pan on the cooling rack for about 5 to 10 minutes before unmolding to cool completely on the same rack.

"WHISKEY AND BEER ARE A MAN'S WORST ENE-MIES... BUT THE MAN THAT RUNS AWAY FROM HIS ENEMIES IS A COWARD!"

Zeca Pagodinho, Brazilian singer

❧ CHEESE BREAD ❧

· Yields 1 Loaf

1	cup whole wheat flour
1	cup all-purpose flour
½	cup finely diced sharp Cheddar cheese
¼	cup sliced scallions
2	teaspoons caraway seeds (optional)
½	cup old-fashioned rolled oats (Quaker Oats)
2	tablespoons sugar
2	teaspoons baking powder
½	teaspoon baking soda
½	teaspoon salt
1½	cups light beer (cold or at room temperature)

Position a rack in the lower third of the oven. Preheat the oven to 400°. In a bowl, thoroughly whisk together the whole wheat flour, all-purpose flour, Cheddar cheese, scallions, caraway seeds, rolled oats, sugar, baking powder, baking soda, and salt. Add the light beer and fold the mixture until the dry ingredients are moistened. Scrape the batter into a loaf pan and spread evenly. Bake the bread for about 35 to 40 minutes until a toothpick inserted in the center and all the way to the bottom of the pan comes out clean.

Let the bread cool in the pan on a cooling rack for about 5 to 10 minutes before unmolding it to cool completely on the same rack.

"I WOULD GIVE ALL MY FAME FOR A POT OF ALE AND SAFETY."

William Shakespeare, English playwright, *King Henry V*

❧{ SOURDOUGH FRENCH BREAD }❧

· Yields 2 Loaves

1	package active dry yeast
12	ounces beer (warmed to 110°)
5	to 5½ cups all-purpose flour
1	cup sourdough starter (room temperature)
3	tablespoons sugar
2	tablespoons butter, softened
2	teaspoons salt
½	teaspoon baking soda
	Water
	Yellow cornmeal

In one bowl, combine the yeast and the warmed beer. Blend in 2 cups of the flour, the sourdough starter, sugar, butter, and salt. In another bowl, combine 1 cup of the flour and the baking soda. Stir this mixture into the flour-yeast mixture. Stir in as much of the remaining flour as possible with the spoon. Knead in enough remaining flour for about 5 to 8 minutes to make a moderately stiff dough that is smooth and elastic. Place the dough into a greased bowl. Turn once. Cover the dough with a cloth towel and let it rise for about 1 to 1½ hours until it is doubled in volume.

Punch down and divide the dough in half. Cover the dough with a cloth towel again and let it rest for 10 minutes.

Shape the dough into 2 round loaves. Place the loaves on a baking sheet. Cover the loaves with cloth towels and let them rise for about 1 hour until they are doubled in volume.

Brush with a little water. Make diagonal slashes across the tops. Sprinkle the cornmeal on top. Bake the loaves at 375° for 30 to 35 minutes.

❖{ RYE BREAD }❖

· Yields 2 Loaves

1¾	cups beer
½	cup molasses (warmed)
2	cakes yeast (dissolved in ¼ cup water)
⅓	cup (5 tablespoons plus 1 teaspoon) butter, softened or melted (plus extra for brushing the dough)
2	teaspoons salt
3	cups rye meal or flour
3	cups all-purpose flour
1	tablespoon caraway seeds

In a bowl, combine the beer and molasses, and add the dissolved yeast. Beat in the rest of the ingredients and blend well. Brush the top of the dough with softened or melted butter, cover with a cloth towel, and let the dough rise until it is doubled in volume.

Punch the dough down, turn it out onto a bread board, and knead it thoroughly for about 7 to 8 minutes, using as much more white flour as is necessary to keep the dough from sticking. Shape the dough into 2 loaves and place them in the loaf pans. Cover the loaves with cloth towels and let them rise until they are doubled in volume.

Bake the loaves at 350° for 35 to 45 minutes or until done.

"THERE IS NOTHING IN THE WORLD LIKE THE FIRST TASTE OF BEER."

John Steinbeck, American novelist

⁍⦃ DINNER ROLLS ⦄⁌

· Yields 1 to 2 dozen

2	cups Bisquick mix
¾	cup beer

In a bowl, combine the Bisquick mix and enough beer to make the dough stiff. Drop tablespoon-size dough onto a baking sheet, leaving 1 to 2 inches between each. Let the dough rise until doubled in volume. Bake at 350° for 20 minutes or until done.

⁍⦃ TWISTS ⦄⁌

· Yields According To Size

½	pound (2 sticks) sweet butter (cold)
2	cups all-purpose flour
1	tablespoon sugar
¾	cup beer

In a bowl, cut the butter into the flour. Add the sugar and beer and mix well. Turn the dough out onto a bread board. Knead the dough until it is no longer sticky. Cover the dough and refrigerate overnight. Tear off chunks of dough the size of a large walnut. Roll each piece between your palms into a 2-inch cylinder. Twist each cylinder 2 or 3 times and place on a cookie sheet. Bake the twists at 400° for 20 minutes.

☀{ WAFFLES }☀

· Yields 8 Waffles

2	cups all-purpose flour
4	eggs, separated
1	teaspoon sugar
5	tablespoons butter, melted
¼	teaspoon salt
½	teaspoon vanilla extract
½	cup light beer
⅔	cup milk
	Powdered sugar

In one bowl, combine the flour, egg yolks, sugar, butter, and salt. Add the vanilla, light beer, and milk. Mix again. In another bowl, beat the egg whites until they are stiff but not dry. Fold the egg whites into the batter. Cook the waffles according to the directions for the waffle iron.

"Boy meets beer. Boy drinks beer. Boy gets another beer. In this performance, the role of the boy will be played by Norm Peterson."

Norm Peterson, Character on "Cheers"

❖⟩ EVERYDAY PANCAKES ⟨❖

· Yields 14 to 16 Pancakes

1	egg, beaten
1	cup milk
¾	cup beer
⅓	cup oil
2	cups packaged pancake mix
1	cup chopped apples or blackberries
	Butter
	Maple-flavored syrup

In one bowl, combine the egg, milk, beer, and oil. Place the pancake mix in another bowl. Add the egg mixture, beating until smooth. Gently fold in the desired fruit. Bake the batter on a hot griddle, using ¼ cup of batter for each pancake. Cook until golden, turning when the pancakes have a bubbly surface and slightly dry edges. If the batter thickens while standing, add a little more beer or milk to achieve the desired consistency.

"You said good friends are hard to come by
I laughed and bought you a beer
it's too corny to cry."

Indigo Girls, American band, "Joking"

⁑{ HOMEMADE PANCAKES }⁑

· Yields 6 Servings

1	cup all-purpose flour
1	teaspoon baking powder
½	teaspoon baking soda
½	teaspoon salt
1	egg
3	tablespoons corn oil
1	tablespoon light molasses
12	ounces beer

In a medium bowl, combine the flour, baking powder, baking soda, and salt, mixing well. In another medium bowl, combine the egg, corn oil, and molasses, mixing well. Add the egg mixture and the beer to the flour mixture, lightly mixing. Heat a griddle to 350°. Spoon 2 tablespoons of batter onto the griddle, spreading the batter into a 3-inch circle with the back of the spoon. Heat each pancake until it is browned on one side and then flip and brown the other side. Serve the Homemade Pancakes with your favorite syrup, butter, and berries.

"AND HERE'S A POT OF GOOD DOUBLE BEER, NEIGHBOUR: DRINK, AND FEAR NOT YOUR MAN."

William Shakespeare, English playwright, *King Henry VI*

❀{ COUNTRY PANCAKES }❀

· Yields 2 Servings

¼	cup (½ stick) butter
¼	cup oat flour
¼	cup graham flour
1	cup whole wheat pastry flour
½	teaspoon baking powder
½	teaspoon baking soda
½	teaspoon salt
1	tablespoon dry malt extract
1	tablespoon sesame seeds
1	cup beer
1½	teaspoons fresh lemon juice

In a skillet, melt the butter. In a large bowl, combine the oat flour, graham flour, whole wheat pastry flour, baking powder, baking soda, salt, dry malt extract, and sesame seeds, mixing well. In a medium bowl, combine the beer and lemon juice, mixing well. Pour the melted butter into the beer mixture, mixing well. Stir the beer mixture into the flour mixture, mixing well. Heat a griddle to 350°. Spoon 2 tablespoons of batter onto the griddle, spreading the batter into a 3-inch circle with the back of the spoon. Heat each pancake until it is browned on one side and then flip and brown the other side. Serve the Country Pancakes with your favorite syrup, butter, and berries.

"GIMME A PIGFOOT AND A BOTTLE OF BEER."

Janis Joplin, American singer

⁘{ BUCKWHEAT PANCAKE ROLLS }⁘

· Yields 4 Servings

⅓	cup buckwheat flour (or more as needed)
⅓	cup all-purpose flour (or more as needed)
2	eggs and 1 yolk
½	cup milk
3	tablespoons beer
	Drop of grappa
¾	cup Bitto cheese (or another semi-soft cheese)
3½	tablespoons cream
½	cup spinach
	Grated Parmesan cheese
⅓	cup (5 tablespoons plus 1 teaspoon) butter
	Sage

In a medium bowl, combine the buckwheat flour, all-purpose flour, eggs, milk, beer, and grappa, mixing well. Let this mixture stand for 30 minutes and then prepare the pancakes in a skillet.

In a pot over steam, melt the Bitto cheese. Add the cream and spinach, mixing well. Spread the cheese mixture onto the pancakes, roll them up, and place them into a greased baking pan. Top the pancake rolls with the Parmesan cheese. Bake the pancake rolls for 10 minutes.

In a skillet, melt the butter and season it with the sage. Brush the sage butter over the pancake rolls before serving them.

"YOU CAN NEVER BUY BEER. YOU JUST RENT IT."

Archie Bunker, Character on "All in the Family"

❧ APPLE TREE PANCAKES ❧

· Yields 2 Servings

1	cup sifted all-purpose flour
1/3	cup sugar + 1/2 teaspoon sugar
1/4	teaspoon salt
1	cup beer (room temperature)
2	egg yolks
4	egg whites
1/4	cup light brown sugar
1 1/2	teaspoons ground cinnamon
2	green apples, peeled, cored, and sliced medium thin
1/2	small lemon
3	tablespoons sweet butter
1	tablespoon vegetable oil

Preheat the oven to 350°. In a large bowl, sift together the flour, 1 1/2 teaspoons of the sugar, and salt. Add the beer, mixing until the batter is smooth. Beat in 1 egg yolk and then the other.

In a medium bowl, beat the egg whites with 1 tablespoon of the sugar until the mixture forms peaks. Fold this egg mixture into the batter.

In a small bowl, combine the remaining sugar, light brown sugar, and cinnamon, mixing well. Reserve 2 teaspoons of this mixture.

Place the apples on a board. Squeeze the lemon over the apples and then coat the apples with the sugar and cinnamon mixture.

In a skillet, heat the sweet butter and vegetable oil. Pour the warm sweet butter and vegetable oil mixture into a casserole dish. Pour half of the batter into the casserole dish and top it with all of the apple slices. Pour the rest of the batter over the apples. Place the batter on the middle oven rack and bake at 350° for 1 hour or until the Apple Tree Pancake is puffy and golden.

Cut the Apple Tree Pancake as desired into smaller pancakes and garnish them with the remaining sugar and cinnamon mixture.

⸭⟩ MICROWAVABLE RYE MUFFINS ⟨⸭

· Yields 12 Muffins

1	cup biscuit mix
1/2	cup rye flour
1	tablespoon sugar
1/4	teaspoon caraway seed
3/4	cup light beer
1	egg
2	tablespoons oil

In a bowl, combine the biscuit mix, rye flour, sugar, and caraway seed. Add the light beer, egg, and oil. Stir until smooth. Spoon the batter into paper-lined microwave muffin cups, filling the cups two-thirds full. Microwave on high, uncovered, 6 muffins at a time for 2 to 2½ minutes or until they are no longer doughy. Rotate the pan once. Repeat with the remaining batter.

THE OLD STONE CROSS
"A STATESMAN IS AN EASY MAN, HE TELLS HIS
LIES BY ROTE.
A JOURNALIST INVENTS HIS LIES, AND RAMS
THEM DOWN YOUR THROAT.
SO STAY AT HOME AND DRINK YOUR BEER AND LET
THE NEIGHBORS VOTE."

William Butler Yeats, Irish poet and playwright

❖{ HUSH PUPPIES }❖

· Yields 1½ Dozen

1¼	cups hush puppy mix
1	7½-ounce can whole tomatoes, drained and chopped
1	small onion, chopped
¼	cup chopped green pepper
¼	teaspoon pepper
¼	teaspoon crushed red pepper
⅛	teaspoon garlic powder
	Pinch of baking powder
1	egg, beaten
⅓	cup beer
	Vegetable oil

In a large bowl, combine all of the ingredients, except the egg, beer, and vegetable oil, mixing well. Create a well in the center of the mixture. In a small bowl, combine the egg and beer, mixing well. Pour the egg mixture into the well of the dry mixture and stir the entire mixture until it is moist.

In a deep fryer, heat the vegetable oil to 375°. Using a tablespoon, drop the batter, a few hush puppies at a time, into the vegetable oil, deep-frying them for approximately 3 to 5 minutes or until they are golden.

"I'VE ALWAYS BELIEVED THAT PARADISE WILL HAVE MY FAVORITE BEER ON TAP."

Rudyard Wheatley, author

⁘{ FRITTER BATTER }⁘

· Yields 1½ Cups

1	cup all-purpose flour
1	egg
1	tablespoon butter, melted
	Dash of salt
½	cup beer
	Vegetables of choice

In a blender, combine all of the ingredients, mixing well until the mixture is smooth. Cover the batter and let it stand for 4 hours. Use the batter with vegetables of choice. Dip the vegetables into the batter and deep-fry them at 360° until they are golden.

"Beer, to begin with, is a food. In Germany, many songs and local proverbs link the name with bread. Bier und Brot. It is more to many drinkers in that it may be considered a specific against many of the ills of the body and mind. It is first a refresher and then a mild stimulant which wipes the cobwebs from dusty minds; it tones up the system, restores circulation, clears the eyes, and brings rose back to faded cheeks."

The Carbon Copy, April 1942

⋅{ PIZZA DOUGH }⋅

· Yields 2 Crusts

1½	teaspoons yeast
2½	cups all-purpose flour
2	teaspoons butter
⅛	teaspoon garlic powder (or to taste)
2	tablespoons oil (plus extra for coating the dough)
2	tablespoons honey
1	cup beer (warm)
	Cornmeal

In a medium bowl, combine all of the ingredients, except the cornmeal, mixing well. Pour the mixture into an electric bread maker. Process the dough on manual, allowing it to rise a little longer after it initially finishes. Separate the dough into two 12-inch pies, rolling them out.

Preheat the oven to 450° to 500°. Place each pie on a cornmeal-coated pizza tin, prick it with a fork, brush it with the extra oil, and add the desired sauce and toppings. For a true Beer Pizza, use the Spaghetti & Pizza Sauce from page 129. Let the pies rise for about 10 to 15 minutes.

Bake the pizzas for approximately 7 minutes until the edges are browned and bubbly.

"DO NOT CEASE TO DRINK BEER, TO EAT, TO INTOXICATE THYSELF, TO MAKE LOVE, AND TO CELEBRATE THE GOOD DAYS."

Ancient Egyptian Credo

CHAPTER 3

Soups & Chili

❊{ AMERICAN CHEESE SOUP }❊

· Yields 3 to 5 Servings

1	cup chicken broth
1/2	cup finely chopped carrots
1/4	cup finely chopped celery
1/4	cup finely chopped onion
1 3/4	cups milk
1/4	cup all-purpose flour
	Dash of pepper
1	cup shredded American cheese
3/4	cup beer

In a saucepan, combine the chicken broth, carrots, celery, and onion. Bring the mixture to a boil and then reduce the heat. Cover and simmer the mixture for 6 to 8 minutes or until the vegetables are tender. In a bowl, combine the milk, flour, and pepper. Stir the milk mixture into the broth and vegetable mixture. Cook and stir until thickened and bubbly. Cook and stir for 1 more minute. Add the American cheese and beer. Stir until the cheese is melted.

"This is grain, which any fool can eat, but for which the Lord intended a more divine means of consumption... Beer!"

Friar Tuck, Character from *Robin Hood, Prince of Thieves*

❧ CHEESE CHOWDER ❧

· Yields 4 Servings

1½	cups small broccoli florets
¾	cup shredded carrots
¾	cup chicken broth or water
¼	cup chopped onion
¼	cup (½ stick) butter
¼	cup all-purpose flour
½	teaspoon dry mustard
¼	teaspoon pepper
2	cups milk
3	ounces cream cheese, cubed and softened
8	ounces Polish sausage or any smoked sausage, fully-cooked and thinly sliced
1½	cups shredded sharp Cheddar or American cheese
¾	cup beer

In a medium saucepan, combine the broccoli, carrots, chicken broth or water, and onion. Bring to a boil. Reduce the heat and simmer, covered, for 8 to 10 minutes or until tender. Do not drain. Set aside.

In a large saucepan, melt the butter. Stir in the flour, dry mustard, and pepper. Add the milk all at once. Cook and stir the mixture until thickened and bubbly. Cook and stir for 1 more minute.

In a bowl, stir about ½ cup of the hot milk mixture into the cream cheese. Stir until well combined. Stir the cream cheese mixture into the remaining milk mixture in the saucepan. Stir the sausage, cheese, and beer into the thickened mixture. Cook and stir over a low heat until the cheese melts and the sausage is heated through. Stir in the undrained vegetables. Heat through.

❧ HAM & VEGETABLE SOUP ❧

· Yields 6 Servings

1¼	cups dry navy beans, rinsed
6	cups water
24	ounces beer
1½	cups water
¾	pound ham hocks (or 1 small meaty ham bone)
1	cup peeled and cubed potatoes
½	cup chopped carrots
½	cup sliced celery
½	cup chopped onion
½	teaspoon crushed dried thyme
⅛	teaspoon pepper
	Few dashes of hot pepper sauce
	Salt and pepper to taste

In a Dutch oven, combine the beans and the 6 cups of water. Bring to a boil, reduce heat, and simmer for 2 minutes. Remove from the heat. Cover the mixture and let it stand for 1 hour. Drain. Add the beer and the 1½ cups of water. Bring to a boil and add the ham hocks. Reduce the heat, cover, and simmer for 1 hour or until the beans are nearly tender.

Remove the ham hocks. Cut the meat off of the bones and coarsely chop. Discard the bones. Return the meat to the soup along with the potatoes, carrots, celery, onion, thyme, pepper, and hot pepper. Cover the mixture and simmer for 30 minutes or until the vegetables are tender. Season with salt and pepper to taste.

"Beauty is in the eye of the beer holder."

Anonymous

⸭⟩ GARDEN PEA SOUP ⟨⸭

· Yields 8 Servings

1	pound green split peas, rinsed and drained
1½	quarts water
2	tablespoons extra virgin olive oil
2	yellow onions, finely chopped
2	carrots, diced
2	celery ribs, diced
5	cups cold water
12	ounces beer
1	meaty ham bone (about 1 pound)
1	medium white potato, peeled and diced
¼	cup chopped fresh parsley
1	teaspoon chopped fresh thyme
½	teaspoon powdered mustard
1	tablespoon cider vinegar
8	ounces fully-cooked bratwurst links or smoked sausage, sliced diagonally
	Salt and pepper to taste

In a saucepan, combine the split peas with the 1½ quarts of water. Soak for 6 to 8 hours or overnight.

Bring the water and peas mixture to a boil for 2 minutes. Remove the mixture from the heat, cover, and let stand for 1 hour. In a stockpot, heat the olive oil over a medium heat. Add the onions, carrots, and celery. Cook, stirring often, for 5 to 7 minutes until the onions are tender. Add the 5 cups of cold water, beer, ham bone, potato, parsley, thyme, powdered mustard, and cider vinegar.

Drain the soaked peas and add them to the pot. Bring to a boil. Reduce the heat to a simmer, cover, and cook for 3 to 4 hours, stirring occasionally, until the peas are tender.

Remove the ham bone. Remove any lean ham and return it to the pot. Discard the fat and bone. Add the bratwurst or smoked sausage and heat through. Add the salt and pepper to taste.

❧ CHILLY CUCUMBER SOUP ❧

· Yields 4 to 6 Servings

12	ounces light beer
½	cup sour cream
2	medium-size cucumbers, finely chopped
1	teaspoon salt
¼	teaspoon garlic powder
½	teaspoon sugar

In a bowl, gradually add the light beer to the sour cream. Add the cucumbers, salt, garlic powder, and sugar. Mix well and serve cold.

"DOUGH... THE STUFF... THAT BUYS ME BEER...
RAY... THE GUY THAT SELLS ME BEER...
ME... THE GUY... WHO DRINKS THE BEER,
FAR... THE DISTANCE TO MY BEER
SO... I THINK I'LL HAVE A BEER...
LA... LA LA LA LA LA LA BEER
TEA... NO THANKS, I'M DRINKING BEER...
            THAT WILL BRING US BACK TO... (LOOKS
            INTO AN EMPTY GLASS)
D'OH!"

Homer J. Simpson, Character on "The Simpsons,"
"Doe Re Mi Beer"

❖{ LENTIL SOUP }❖

· Yields 8 to 10 Servings

2	cups dried lentils
4	cups beer
4	cups water
4	cups chicken broth
1	meaty ham bone
2	tablespoons butter
2	medium onions, minced
2	ribs celery, very thinly sliced
3	medium carrots, very thinly sliced
	Salt and pepper to taste

In a saucepan, cover the lentils in water and soak overnight. Drain the lentils and pour them into a kettle. Stir the beer, 4 cups of water, and broth into the kettle. Add the ham bone and bring the mixture to a boil. Reduce the heat and simmer the lentils, covered, for 3 hours, stirring occasionally. Remove the ham bone, strip off the meat, break the meat into small pieces, and return the meat to the kettle. In a skillet, melt the butter over a medium heat. Add the onions, celery, and carrots and sauté them for 10 minutes or until they are softened but not browned. With a slotted spoon, transfer the vegetables to the soup kettle and cook the soup for 30 more minutes. Season the soup with the salt and pepper to taste.

"MILK IS FOR BABIES. WHEN YOU GROW UP
YOU HAVE TO DRINK BEER."
Arnold Schwarzenegger, Austrian-American actor and statesman

❧{ BEAN SOUP }❧

· Yields 6 Servings

2	15-ounce cans pinto beans, drained and rinsed
½	cup beer
½	medium onion, sliced
3	cloves garlic, minced
½	cup chopped fresh cilantro
1	fresh jalapeño pepper, thinly sliced

In a saucepan, combine all of the ingredients, mixing well. Simmer the mixture, uncovered, over a low heat for 30 minutes.

"FILL WITH MINGLED CREAM AND AMBER,
I WILL DRAIN THAT GLASS AGAIN.
SUCH HILARIOUS VISIONS CLAMBER
THROUGH THE CHAMBER OF MY BRAIN.
QUAINTEST THOUGHTS, QUEEREST FANCIES
COME TO LIFE AND FADE AWAY.
WHAT CARE I HOW TIME ADVANCES:
I AM DRINKING ALE TODAY."

Edgar Allen Poe, American poet

❧ BROCCOLI CHEESE SOUP ❧

· Yields 10 Servings

2	14.5-ounce cans vegetable broth (or chicken broth)
1	small onion, chopped
¼	teaspoon garlic powder
¼	teaspoon white pepper
	Seasoned salt to taste
	Cayenne pepper to taste
1	pound broccoli, chopped (fresh or frozen)
¾	cup (1½ sticks) butter
	All-purpose flour
4	cups milk
2	pounds Cheddar cheese, cubed or shredded
2	ounces beer

In a large pot, combine the broth and onion, bringing the mixture to a boil. Add the seasonings and half of the broccoli, bringing the mixture to a boil again. Then simmer. In a frying pan, make a roux by melting the butter. Whisk the flour into the melted butter until thick. Stir the roux into the soup and whisk it. In another saucepan, combine the milk and Cheddar cheese, continually stirring and heating the mixture until the cheese melts. Blend the cheese mixture into the soup mixture, mixing well. Add the beer, mixing well. Add the remaining broccoli, continuing to stir.

"WHY BEER IS BETTER THAN WINE: '... HUMAN FEET ARE CONSPICUOUSLY ABSENT FROM BEER MAKING.'"

Steve Mirsky, *Scientific American* (May, 2007)

❧ BACON & CHEDDAR SOUP ❧

· Yields 12 Servings

6	ounces vegetable oil
1½	pounds onions, chopped
1¼	pounds potatoes, diced
1	pound carrots, diced
1	pound celery, sliced
1	1-pound jar double Cheddar cheese sauce
½	pound bacon, cooked and crumbled
2	cups beer
1	quart chicken stock
1¼	pounds frozen mixed vegetables
½	teaspoon paprika
½	teaspoon white pepper
¼	teaspoon liquid smoke
2	tablespoons chopped fresh parsley

In a large pot, combine the vegetable oil, onions, potatoes, carrots, and celery, mixing well. Sauté the mixture for 30 minutes or until the vegetables are tender. Add the remaining ingredients, mixing well. Simmer the mixture, uncovered, for 20 minutes over a low heat, lightly stirring.

"There is more to life than beer alone, but beer makes those other things even better."

Stephen Morris, English musician

❖{ ONION & CHEDDAR SOUP }❖

· Yields 6 Servings

4	tablespoons unsalted butter
4	medium onions, peeled and sliced
4	cups low-sodium beef broth
1/8	teaspoon freshly grated nutmeg
12	ounces beer
1/2	pound sharp Cheddar cheese, shredded
	Salt and freshly ground pepper to taste

In a large pot, melt the butter. Add the onions and cook the mixture, covered, for 15 minutes. Uncover the pot and continue to sauté the onions, stirring frequently, for about 35 minutes until they are golden. Add the broth and nutmeg. Cover the mixture and bring it to a boil. Reduce the heat and simmer the mixture, uncovered, for 15 minutes. In a small pot, bring the beer to a boil over a medium heat until it is reduced by half. Remove the beer from the heat and add the Cheddar cheese, stirring until the cheese melts. Pour the melted Cheddar cheese mixture into a blender, adding 1 cup of the soup mixture and blending until the mixture is smooth. Set this mixture aside. Remove the soup mixture from the heat and strain the liquid. Reserve this liquid. In a blender, purée the strained onions until they are very smooth. Pour the puréed onions into the soup pot. Add the reserved liquid and the Cheddar cheese mixture. Add the salt and pepper to taste.

"GOD HAS A BROWN VOICE, AS SOFT AND FULL AS BEER."

Anne Sexton, American poet

❄⟩ REUBEN SOUP ⟨❄

· Yields 8 Servings

1	corned beef brisket (3 to 4 pounds), rinsed
2	cups rinsed and drained sauerkraut
3	cups thinly sliced red cabbage
12	ounces beer
2	medium onions, thinly sliced
4	cloves garlic, chopped
3	tablespoons Dijon mustard
3	tablespoons butter
3	tablespoons all-purpose flour
3	tablespoons tomato paste
1	tablespoon mild paprika
2	teaspoons caraway seed
	Salt and pepper to taste
10	slices pumpernickel bread, cubed and toasted
2	cups shredded Swiss cheese

In a Dutch oven, cover the corned beef brisket with cold water, bring the water to a boil, and skim off any matter that rises to the surface. Reduce the heat to low and simmer the meat, covered, for 3½ hours.

Remove the meat from the stock, cool the meat, trim away all fat, and cut into 1-inch cubes. Set the meat aside.

In the Dutch oven, measure out 8 cups of the stock, discarding the rest. Pour 7 of those cups back into the Dutch oven and bring the stock to a boil. Reserve the last cup of stock. Add the sauerkraut, cabbage, beer, onions, garlic, and mustard, mixing well. Bring the mixture to a boil and then simmer the mixture, covered, for approximately 20 minutes or until the cabbage is tender.

In a large skillet, melt the butter, stir in the flour, and cook the mixture, uncovered, over a medium heat for 2 minutes or until the flour is a light tan color.

Stir in the tomato paste and the remaining cup of reserved stock. Stir in the paprika and caraway seed. Stir the mixture until it becomes thick. Pour this seasoning sauce into the Dutch oven. Add the salt and pepper to taste. Add the corned beef, cooking the mixture, covered, for about 5 minutes or until it is thoroughly heated. Garnish each serving with the pumpernickel and Swiss cheese.

⋅⅊ STUFFED PEPPER SOUP ⅊⋅

· Yields 10 to 12 Servings

2	pounds ground beef
2	cups rice (if using Minute Rice, cook and let stand for 5 minutes)
2	cups chopped green pepper
1	cup chopped onion
1	28-ounce can diced tomatoes
1	28-ounce can tomato sauce
2	cubes beef bouillon
1	14- to 16-ounce can beef broth
12	ounces beer
½	cup ketchup
¼	cup packed brown sugar

In a large pot, combine all of the ingredients, mixing well. Simmer, stirring occasionally, until the peppers and onions are soft. This could take several hours.

"THE GOVERNMENT WILL FALL THAT RAISES THE PRICE OF BEER."

Czech saying

❧ WILD RICE SOUP ❧

· Yields 6 Servings

¼	cup olive oil
1	medium yellow onion, chopped
1	medium red onion, chopped
1	bunch green onions, chopped
8	shallots, chopped
5	cloves garlic, minced
3	cups carrots, chopped
2	quarts beef or chicken broth
⅓	cup honey
18	ounces beer
1	quart wild rice (cooked)
	Salt and pepper to taste

In a skillet, combine the olive oil, onions, shallots, and garlic, sautéing until the mixture is browned. In a large pot, combine the onion mixture with the carrots, broth, and honey, mixing well. Bring the mixture to a boil. Add the beer, stirring well. Add the rice and simmer the mixture, uncovered, for 15 minutes. Season with the salt and pepper to taste.

"THE HOUSE WAS AS EMPTY AS A BEER CLOSET IN PREMISES WHERE PAINTERS HAVE BEEN AT WORK."

Mark Twain, American author

❖{ CHEESE BISQUE }❖

· Yields 4 Servings

¼	cup (½ stick) butter
1	small onion, chopped
2	small carrots, chopped
½	cup chopped celery
⅓	cup all-purpose flour
3	cups light cream
1	cup beer
2½	cups grated sharp Cheddar cheese
4	egg yolks, lightly beaten
	Salt to taste
	White pepper to taste
	Sour cream
¼	cup chopped chives to taste

In a large pot, combine the butter, onion, carrots, and celery, sautéing the vegetables until they are golden. Stir in the flour. Slowly stir in the cream and beer. Cook the mixture over a low heat, stirring constantly until the mixture is slightly thickened. Add the Cheddar cheese, stirring until the cheese is melted. In a large bowl, beat the soup mixture into the egg yolks. Return the soup mixture to the pot and heat until desired doneness. Add the salt and white pepper to taste. Garnish each serving with a dollop of sour cream and sprinkling of chives.

"I WORK UNTIL BEER O'CLOCK."

Stephen King, American author

❊{ CHEESEY SOUP }❊

· Yields 10 Servings

1	cup chopped cooked bacon, drippings reserved
½	cup chopped green bell pepper
1	cup chopped celery
½	medium onion, chopped
⅔	cup all-purpose flour
½	cup (1 stick) butter
3	quarts milk
1	2-ounce jar pimiento, drained and chopped
1	cup chicken bouillon
½	teaspoon garlic powder
1½	pounds Cheddar cheese, grated
½	pound Provolone cheese, grated
½	cup beer
¼	cup chopped parsley
	Salt and pepper to taste

In a skillet, combine ¾ teaspoon of the reserved bacon drippings, bell pepper, celery, and onion, sautéing the vegetables until they are browned.

In a large saucepan, create a roux by combining the flour and butter over a low heat. When the roux mixture begins to brown, add the milk, mixing well. Add the vegetable mixture, bacon, pimiento, bouillon, and garlic powder, mixing well, and heat the mixture over a medium heat. When the mixture is warm, add the Cheddar and Provolone cheeses, stirring until the cheeses melt. Add the beer to the soup. Reduce the heat and simmer the mixture, covered, for 20 minutes.

Garnish each serving with the parsley. Season with salt and pepper to taste.

❖{ HOT SAUCE SOUP }❖

· Yields 10 Servings

6	cups milk
24	ounces beer
40	ounces processed cheese spread
10	ounces chicken broth
1	teaspoon Worcestershire sauce
3	dashes hot sauce (or to taste)
¼	cup + 2 tablespoons cornstarch
	Garlic or onion croutons

In a Dutch oven, combine the milk and 18 ounces of the beer, mixing well. Heat the mixture over a low heat, stirring constantly, until thoroughly heated. Add the cheese spread, broth, Worcestershire sauce, and hot sauce, mixing well. Cook the mixture over a low heat, stirring constantly, until thoroughly heated. In a small bowl, combine the cornstarch and the remaining 6 ounces of beer, mixing well. Add this mixture to the cheese mixture, mixing well. Simmer the mixture, uncovered, stirring constantly, until it is thickened but do not boil it. Garnish each serving with the croutons.

"Beer makes you feel the way you ought to feel without beer."
Henry Lawson, Australian writer and poet

᪥᪥{ SEAFOOD GUMBO }᪥᪥

· Yields 12 Servings

³/₄	cup oil
³/₄	cup all-purpose flour
2	cloves garlic, minced
2	cups chopped yellow onions
³/₄	cup chopped bell pepper
3	bay leaves
¹/₂	teaspoon Old Bay Seasoning
¹/₂	teaspoon cayenne pepper
¹/₂	teaspoon salt
2	cups oysters and their liquid
6	cups fish or shrimp broth
1	16-ounce can tomatoes, half the liquid drained, diced
6	ounces beer
1¹/₂	pounds white meat fish fillets, cut into 3-inch pieces
1	pound medium shrimp, peeled and deveined
¹/₂	cup minced fresh parsley

In a large pot, combine the oil and flour, whisking well to create a roux. Cook the roux over a medium heat, stirring constantly, until the mixture becomes light brown. Add the garlic, onions, bell pepper, bay leaves, Old Bay Seasoning, cayenne pepper, and salt, mixing well. Cook this mixture, uncovered, for 10 to 15 minutes.

Add the oyster liquid, broth, tomatoes, and beer, mixing well. Cook this mixture, uncovered, for 40 minutes.

Add the fish fillets and cook for 3 minutes. Add the shrimp and cook for 3 minutes. Add the oysters and cook for 5 minutes. Fold in the parsley. Cover the pot, remove it from the heat, and let it stand for 5 minutes.

Remove the bay leaves before serving.

∗{ BEER CHILI }∗

· Yields 4 Servings

2	tablespoons oil
2	pounds beef chuck or round, cut into ½-inch pieces
1	cup chopped onions
3	tablespoons ground cumin
1	tablespoon paprika
3	tablespoons chili powder or 1 to 2 teaspoons cayenne pepper
1	tablespoon ground celery seed
1	tablespoon oregano
1	tablespoon chopped garlic
½	small fresh chili pepper, finely chopped
1	bay leaf
1	cup beer
1½	cups tomato purée
1½	cups beef broth
3	cups cooked kidney or chili beans
	Salt and pepper to taste
2	tablespoons chopped fresh parsley or fresh cilantro

In a Dutch oven, heat the oil over a moderately high heat. When the oil is very hot, add enough of the beef to cover the bottom of the Dutch oven without crowding and sear the meat on all sides. Remove the meat with a slotted spoon and repeat until you have seared all the meat.

Lower the heat to moderate and cook the onions for 5 to 7 minutes until they soften. Add the cumin, paprika, chili powder, celery seed, oregano, and garlic to the Dutch oven and cook, stirring, for 2 minutes. Add all of the remaining ingredients, except the parsley, and bring them to a boil over a high heat. Reduce the heat to low, cover the Dutch oven, and cook for 1½ hours or until the meat is tender. Garnish with the parsley.

❧ BEEF & PORK CHILI ❧

· Yields 8 Servings

1½	pounds boneless beef top round, trimmed of fat and cut into 1-inch cubes
1	pound lean boneless pork (from the leg or loin), trimmed of fat and cut into 1-inch cubes
1½	cups beer
2	medium onions, chopped
2	cloves garlic, minced
¼	cup masa flour (corn tortilla flour)
1	28-ounce can tomatoes
2	tablespoons chili powder
1	teaspoon ground cumin
1	teaspoon dry oregano
½	cup chopped cilantro
1	7-ounce can green chile salsa
1	medium jalapeño pepper, seeded and finely chopped
1	large green bell pepper, seeded and finely chopped
2	tablespoons lemon juice
	Salt to taste

In a kettle, combine the beef, pork, and ½ cup of the beer, mixing well. Cook the mixture, covered, over a medium heat for 30 minutes. Simmer the mixture, covered, for 30 minutes. Add the onions and garlic, continuing to cook the mixture, uncovered, for approximately 30 minutes until most of the liquid evaporates and the juices and onions are browned.

Add the masa flour, gently stirring the mixture for 30 seconds. Blend in the remaining 1 cup of beer. Add the tomatoes and their juice, chili powder, cumin, oregano, cilantro, salsa, jalapeño pepper, and bell pepper, mixing well. Reduce the heat and simmer the mixture, covered, for approximately 1½ hours until the beef is tender.

Stir in the lime juice and add the salt to taste.

❧ VEGETARIAN CHILI ❧

· Yields 4 to 6 Serving

2	tablespoons olive oil
1	small onion, diced
3	cloves garlic, minced
1	jalapeño pepper, seeded and diced
1	chile pepper, seeded and diced
1	15-ounce can black beans (with the juice)
3	Roma tomatoes, cut into eighths
¼	cup cashews
1	teaspoon cumin
1	teaspoon chili powder
½	teaspoon ground cinnamon
¼	teaspoon cayenne pepper
¼	teaspoon red pepper flakes
6	ounces beer
¼	16-ounce can frozen corn
2	heads broccoli, steamed
	Shredded Cheddar cheese

In a skillet, combine the olive oil, onion, and garlic, sautéing the onions until they become translucent. Add the jalapeño pepper and chile pepper, continuing to sauté for a few more minutes. Add the beans, tomatoes, cashews, cumin, chili powder, cinnamon, cayenne pepper, red pepper flakes, and beer, mixing well. Bring the mixture to a boil. Continue to boil the mixture, stirring frequently, for approximately 35 minutes until most of the liquid has evaporated.

Add the corn about 10 to 15 minutes before the mixture is ready to be served.

Garnish the Vegetarian Chili with the broccoli and Cheddar cheese.

❖⟨ VENISON CHILI ⟩❖

· Yields 8 to 10 Servings

5	pounds venison (leg or shoulder roast), cut into ½-inch cubes
½	cup chili powder
2½	pounds smoked sausage
3½	pounds onions, chopped
1½	cups masa flour (corn tortilla flour)
7½	cups beer
6	pounds canned tomatoes (with the liquid)
1	quart chicken stock
½	cup chopped garlic
¼	cup dried oregano
3	tablespoons ground cumin
1½	tablespoons salt
1	tablespoon pepper

In a large bowl, combine the venison and chili powder, tossing to mix well. Cover and marinate the venison at room temperature for 2 to 3 hours.

In a kettle, remove the casings from the sausage and crumble. Add the venison and onions. Cook and stir the mixture until the venison is browned and the onions are translucent. Mix in the masa flour and cook the mixture, stirring constantly, for about 3 minutes. Add the beer, tomatoes, chicken stock, garlic, oregano, cumin, salt, and pepper, mixing well. Bring the mixture to a boil. Reduce the heat and simmer the mixture, uncovered, for approximately 2½ to 3 hours until the venison is tender and the sauce is thick.

"FOR A QUART OF ALE IS A DISH FOR A KING."

William Shakespeare, English playwright, *A Winter's Tale*

CHAPTER 4

Salads

❧ BEER DRESSING OVER GREEN SALAD ❧

· Yields 6 to 8 Servings

For the salad:

6	cups water
3	carrots, cut into 1-inch pieces
1	cup cauliflower florets
1	cup broccoli florets
1/2	cup thinly sliced fresh mushrooms
1	cup firmly packed spinach leaves, washed, stemmed, and patted dry
1	cup firmly packed bite-size pieces romaine lettuce

For the dressing:

1/2	cup mayonnaise
1/4	cup Dijon mustard
1/4	cup beer
1	tablespoon horseradish
2	drops hot pepper sauce (optional)

In a saucepan, boil the water. Place the carrots into the boiling water. Lower the heat to medium and simmer the carrots for 5 minutes. With a slotted spoon, transfer the carrots to paper towels to drain. Bring the water to a boil again, add the cauliflower, and cook it for 5 minutes. Transfer the cauliflower to paper towels to drain.

Bring the water to another boil, add the broccoli, and cook it for 5 minutes. Transfer the broccoli to paper towels to drain.

In a large serving bowl, combine the carrots, cauliflower, broccoli, mushrooms, spinach, and romaine lettuce.

In a medium bowl, combine the mayonnaise, mustard, beer, and horseradish to create the Beer Dressing. Stir in the hot pepper sauce, if desired. Spoon the dressing over the vegetables and toss the salad well.

ᪧᴥ{ DANDELION SALAD }ᴥᪧ

· Yields 4 Servings

4	cups young, tender dandelion greens
2	hard-boiled eggs, chopped
4	slices bacon, cut up
1/3	cup beer
1	tablespoon honey

In a bowl, combine the dandelion greens and eggs. Set aside. In a skillet, fry the bacon and then remove from the heat. Stir the beer and honey into the bacon and drippings. Pour the dressing over the salad and toss well.

ᪧᴥ{ COLESLAW }ᴥᪧ

· Yields 12 Servings

8	cups shredded green cabbage
1/2	medium-size green bell pepper, chopped
1 1/2	tablespoons minced onion
1	cup mayonnaise
1/4	cup beer
1	teaspoon celery seed
1/2	teaspoon salt
1/4	teaspoon freshly ground pepper

In a large bowl, combine the cabbage, bell pepper, and onion.

In a small bowl, combine the mayonnaise, beer, celery seed, salt, and pepper. Pour the beer mixture over the cabbage mixture and toss to coat.

Refrigerate the coleslaw for at least 30 minutes before serving.

❧ POTATO SALAD ❧

· Yields 4 Servings

6	medium potatoes
4	slices bacon
1	tablespoon chopped onion
1	rib celery, chopped
1	teaspoon salt
2	tablespoons butter
2	tablespoons unbleached flour
½	teaspoon dry mustard
1	tablespoon sugar
1	cup beer
½	teaspoon Tabasco sauce
2	tablespoons chopped fresh parsley

In a medium saucepan, boil the potatoes until they are tender. In a skillet, fry the bacon until it is crisp. In a medium bowl, break the bacon into small pieces and combine it with the onion, celery, and salt. Set this mixture aside. In a small saucepan, combine the butter and flour, mixing well until the butter is melted. Add the mustard and sugar and stir in the beer and Tabasco sauce. Bring the mixture to a boil, stirring constantly. Pour this mixture over the potatoes. Sprinkle with the parsley. Toss the salad and let it stand for 1 hour. Add the bacon mixture. Toss the salad once more before serving.

"Flow Welsted, flow! like thine inspirer, beer!
Tho' stale, not ripe; tho' thin, yet never clear;
So sweetly mawkish, and so smoothly dull;
Heady, not strong; o'erflowing tho' not full."

Alexander Pope, English poet

CHAPTER 5

Vegetables

❧ GREEN BEANS ❧

· Yields 4 Servings

1	pound green beans
¼	cup beer
2	tablespoons chopped onion
¼	teaspoon prepared horseradish
½	teaspoon dry mustard
¼	teaspoon salt
	Dash of pepper

Drain the green beans and place in one bowl. In another bowl, combine the beer, onions, horseradish, mustard, salt, and pepper. Pour the beer mixture over the green beans to cover. Cover and marinate in the refrigerator for 30 minutes. Drain and serve.

❧ CARROTS ❧

· Yields 4 Servings

1	tablespoon butter
1	cup beer
4	large carrots, peeled and sliced into long, thin slices
¼	teaspoon salt
1	teaspoon sugar

In a skillet, melt the butter. Add the beer and the carrots. Slowly cook the mixture, stirring frequently, until the carrots are tender. Stir in the salt and sugar. Cook for another 2 minutes.

❖{ Glazed Carrots }❖

· Yields 6 to 8 Servings

3	cups sliced carrots
2	cups salted water
2	slices bacon
½	cup chopped green pepper
¼	cup chopped onion
1	teaspoon cornstarch
⅓	cup beer
½	teaspoon sugar
½	teaspoon crushed dried basil
⅛	teaspoon salt
⅛	teaspoon crushed dried rosemary
2	tablespoons snipped fresh parsley

In a covered saucepan, cook the carrots in the boiling salted water for 15 to 20 minutes or until they are crispy yet tender. Drain. In a skillet, cook the bacon until it is crisp. Remove the bacon, reserving 1 tablespoon of drippings in the skillet. Crumble the bacon and set aside.

In the skillet, cook the green pepper and onion in the reserved drippings until they are tender, but not brown. Slowly blend in the cornstarch. Add the beer to the skillet along with the sugar, basil, salt, and rosemary. Cook and stir until bubbly. Continue to cook and stir for 1 more minute. Stir in the cooked carrots. Heat through. Sprinkle the mixture with the crumbled bacon and parsley.

"There is no such thing as a bad beer. It's that some taste better than others."

Billy Carter, Brother of President Jimmy Carter

❧ FRIED POTATOES ❧

· Yields 2 Servings

1	tablespoon butter
2	tablespoons beer
1	large sweet onion, cut into ¼-inch squares
	Seasoned salt to taste
	Pepper to taste
2	medium potatoes, cut into small slices (or use 1 to 2 cans sliced potatoes, drained)
	Salt to taste
	Parsley flakes as desired

In a frying pan, melt the butter and add the beer, allowing it to coat the surface of the frying pan. Add the onions, seasoned salt, and pepper and slowly fry for 3 to 4 minutes until the onions are soft. Add the potato slices to the frying pan, seasoning them with additional seasoned salt and pepper to taste. Stir the potatoes around, coating them with the beer and butter. Fry the potatoes until the juices are absorbed and fried-up. Season the potatoes with the salt and pepper to taste. Sprinkle the parsley flakes on top of the potatoes.

"MMMMMM, BEER."

Homer J. Simpson, Character on "The Simpsons"

⁖{ POTATO & CABBAGE CASSEROLE }⁖

· Yields 4 Servings

1½	pounds potatoes, unpeeled
½	pound bacon, cut into 3-inch strips
1	cup sliced onion
2	tablespoons all-purpose flour
½	teaspoon dried thyme
½	teaspoon salt
12	ounces beer
½	cup milk
6	cups shredded cabbage
1	cup shredded Swiss cheese

In a saucepan, steam the potatoes in 1-inch of boiling water for 30 to 40 minutes or until they are tender.

Slice the potatoes into ½-inch slices and set them aside.

In a large skillet, fry the bacon until it is crisp and set it aside. Pour off all but 2 tablespoons of the bacon fat and sauté the onions in the skillet. Stir in the flour, thyme, and salt. Add the beer and milk, stirring the mixture over a low heat until it boils and thickens.

Preheat the oven to 375°.

In a casserole dish, layer half of the cabbage, potatoes, bacon, Swiss cheese, and beer sauce. Repeat the layering with the other half of the remaining ingredients. Bake the mixture, covered, for 30 minutes.

Uncover the casserole dish and bake the mixture for 15 minutes or until the cabbage is tender.

❧ PINTO BEANS ❧

· Yields 8 Servings

1	pound dry pinto beans, rinsed
1	pound smoked ham hocks
7	cups water
12	ounces beer
½	cup chopped onion
16	ounces tomatoes, diced
3	tablespoons molasses
1	teaspoon dry mustard
¼	teaspoon pepper

In a saucepan, combine the beans, ham hocks, and water and bring to a boil. Cover and let simmer for 1 hour, stirring occasionally. Remove the ham hocks and cut the meat from the bone. Add the beer and onions. Return the meat to the beans along with the tomatoes, molasses, dry mustard, and pepper. Cover and simmer for 1 more hour or until the beans are tender, stirring occasionally. Add additional beer or water, if necessary.

"MIKE HAMMER DRINKS BEER BECAUSE I CAN'T SPELL COGNAC."

Mickey Spillane, American detective novelist

❧ SAUERKRAUT ❧

· Yields 6 to 8 Servings

1	pound sauerkraut
12	ounces beer
2	to 3 tablespoons brown sugar (optional)
6	to 8 links smoked sausage

In a bowl, combine all of the ingredients. Place the mixture into a casserole dish and cover with foil. Bake at 350° for 1½ hours.

❧ BRUSSELS SPROUTS ❧

· Yields 4 Servings

1	pound fresh Brussels sprouts, trimmed, and washed
	Beer
½	teaspoon salt
2	tablespoons butter

In a medium saucepan, cover the brussels sprouts with the beer. Bring the mixture to a boil, reduce the heat, and simmer it, covered, for approximately 20 minutes or until the brussels sprouts are tender. Drain the brussels sprouts. Add the salt and butter.

❧ ONION RINGS ❧

· Yields 2 Servings

1⅓	cups all-purpose flour
1	teaspoon salt
¼	teaspoon pepper
1	tablespoon oil
2	egg yolks
¾	cup beer
2	large white onions, sliced ¼-inch thick

In a medium bowl, combine the flour, salt, pepper, oil, and egg yolks, mixing well. Whisk in the beer. Refrigerate the batter for 3½ hours before using.

Dip the onion slices into the batter, coating them completely. Deep-fry the onion slices at 375° until they are golden brown.

"Here's a toast to the roast that good fellowship lends, with the sparkle of beer and wine; may its sentiment always be deeper, my friends, than the foam at the top of the stein."

Ogden Nash, American poet

ᐧᐧ{ CABBAGE }ᐧᐧ

· Yields 2 to 4 Servings

2	tablespoons butter
1/4	head cabbage (outer leaves removed), cut into 1/2-inch slices
1/3	cup beer
1/8	teaspoon salt
	Pepper to taste
1	teaspoon sugar

In a skillet, melt the butter. Add the cabbage to the skillet and cook for 3 minutes. Add the beer, salt, pepper, and sugar. Continue to cook for 5 minutes. Drain and serve hot.

"It doesn't matter if you're black
It doesn't matter if you're white
Take a dollar fifty
A six pack of beer
And we goin' dance all night."

The Rolling Stones, English band, "Going To A Go Go"

☙ FRIED VEGETABLES ❧

· Yields 4 Servings

1	1-ounce envelope onion soup mix
1	cup unbleached all-purpose flour
1	teaspoon baking powder
2	large eggs
1	tablespoon prepared mustard
½	cup beer
4	to 5 cups vegetables of choice (examples: broccoli florets, cauliflower florets, sliced mushrooms, or sliced zucchini)

In a large bowl, combine the soup mix, flour, baking powder, eggs, mustard, and beer, beating the mixture until it is smooth. Let the batter stand for 10 minutes.

Dip the vegetables into the batter, coating them completely. Deep-fry the vegetables at 375° until they are golden brown. Drain the vegetables on paper towels before serving.

"Last night I dreamed that I passed from the scene
And I went to a place so sublime
Aw, the water was clear and tasted like beer
Then they turned it all into wine."

Tom T. Hall, American country music singer, "I Like Beer"

❖{ ZUCCHINI }❖

· Yields 4 Servings

1½	cups all-pupose flour
1	teaspoon baking powder
¼	teaspoon seasoned salt
6	to 8 ounces beer
1	egg
3	teaspoons seasoned salt (or favorite seasoning)
1	teaspoon pepper
2	zucchini, halved or quartered
	Oil for frying

In a bowl, combine the flour, baking powder, and the ¼ teaspoon of seasoned salt, mixing well. Pour in the beer and add the egg, whisking the mixture until it is smooth. Let the batter stand for approximately 15 to 20 minutes.

Combine the 3 teaspoons of seasoned salt and pepper. Toss the zucchini pieces in the seasonings to coat.

In a skillet, heat the oil to 350°. Add the zucchini to the beer batter, coating the pieces. Fry the zucchini pieces in the oil for approximately 1½ to 2 minutes or until they are golden. Drain the zucchini on paper towels. Serve with your favorite dipping sauce.

"AN OPPRESSIVE GOVERNMENT IS MORE TO BE FEARED THAN A TIGER, OR A BEER."

Confucius, Chinese philosopher

❖⟨ SIDE DISH RICE ⟩❖

· Yields 2 Servings

2½	tablespoons olive oil
1	cup raw long grain rice
1	10¾-ounce can condensed onion soup
10¾	ounces beer

In a saucepan, heat the olive oil over a medium heat. Add the rice and lightly brown, stirring constantly. Add the soup and beer, mixing well. Simmer the mixture, covered, for about 25 minutes or until all of the liquid is absorbed.

"LET OTHER MORTALS VAINLY WEAR
A TEDIOUS LIFE IN ANXIOUS CARE;
LET THE AMBITIOUS TOIL AND THINK,
LET STATES OR EMPIRES SWIM OR SINK;
MY SOLE AMBITION IS TO DRINK."

Anonymous

❧ WILD RICE ❧

· Yields 6 Servings

½	cup wild rice
¾	cup beer
¼	teaspoon salt
½	cup water
4	slices bacon
1	cup sliced fresh mushrooms
1	cup shredded carrots
½	cup chopped onion

Place the rice into a strainer. Run cold water over the rice for 1 minute, lifting the rice to rinse well. In a saucepan, combine the rice, beer, salt, and water. Boil. Cover and simmer for 40 to 50 minutes.

In a frying pan, fry the bacon until it is crisp. Drain, reserving 2 tablespoons of drippings. Crumble the bacon and set it aside.

In another saucepan, combine and cook the mushrooms, carrots, and onions in the bacon drippings until they are tender. Stir the rice mixture into the vegetable mixture and thoroughly heat. Transfer to a serving bowl, and sprinkle the mixture with bacon.

"THE SECRET OF DRUNKENESS IS, THAT IT INSULATES US IN THOUGHT, WHILST IT UNITES US IN FEELING."

Ralph Waldo Emerson, American poet

⋆⟨ BAKED BEANS ⟩⋆

· Yields 8 Servings

1	pound navy beans
12	ounces beer
½	pound bacon
1	onion
2	tablespoons firmly packed dark brown sugar
2	tablespoons molasses
2	tablespoons ketchup
2	teaspoons mustard
1	teaspoon salt

In a medium saucepan, cover the navy beans with water and heat the mixture over a medium heat. Bring the mixture to a boil, cover, remove it from the heat, and let the beans stand for 1 hour. Drain the beans, rinse them, and drain them again. Pour the beans into a casserole dish.

In a medium bowl, combine all of the other ingredients, mixing well. Pour this mixture over the beans in the casserole dish. Add enough water to just cover the beans. Bake the beans, covered, at 275° for 5 hours. Add water as needed to keep the beans covered.

Uncover the casserole dish and bake the beans at 275° for 30 to 60 minutes until the mixture is thickened.

"Let us drink for the replenishment of our strength, not for our sorrow."

Cicero, Roman statesman and philosopher

❧ SUMMER BARBECUE BEANS ❧

· Yields 8 Servings

2	16-ounce cans pork and beans
8	ounces beer
1	cup ketchup
1	cup firmly packed dark brown sugar
¼	cup dehydrated onions
	Hotdogs, sliced

In a medium bowl, combine all of the ingredients, mixing well. Pour the mixture into a casserole dish. Bake the mixture, covered, at 325° for 1 hour or until the liquid is cooked away and the beans are firm.

❧ ASPARAGUS ❧

· Yields 3 to 4 Servings

1	cup all-purpose flour
	Salt and pepper to taste
	Garlic powder to taste
	Seasoned salt to taste
	Italian seasoning to taste
2	ounces beer
1½	pounds asparagus, cut into 2-inch pieces
	Olive oil

In a small bowl, combine the flour and seasonings, mixing well. Add the beer, mixing until the mixture is thick. Roll the asparagus spears in the flour mixture, coating them completely. Deep-fry the asparagus spears in 2-inches of the olive oil until they are golden brown.

❋{ MARINATED VEGETABLES }❋

· Yields 4 to 8 Servings

1	medium cucumber, thinly sliced
1	medium green pepper, cut into strips
1	medium zucchini or squash, cut into bite-size pieces
1	cup cauliflower florets
1	cup broccoli florets
1	cup fresh mushroom halves
1	cup cherry tomatoes
1/2	cup beer
1/4	cup extra virgin olive oil
2	tablespoons balsamic vinegar
3/4	teaspoon dried basil
3/4	teaspoon dill seed or dill weed
1/2	teaspoon salt
1	teaspoon Dijon mustard
	Dash of seasoned pepper (or to taste)
	Seasoned salt to taste
	Garlic powder to taste

In a storage container, combine all of the vegetables.

In a bowl, combine the beer and remaining ingredients. Pour the beer marinade over the vegetables. Cover and chill for at least 4 hours.

CHAPTER 6

Fruit

{ AVOCADO WEDGES }

· Yields 2 Servings

1	cup beer
1	cup all-purpose flour
1½	teaspoons paprika
2	cloves garlic, chopped
2	avocados, peeled and cut into 6 wedges
	Salt to taste
	Salsa

In a medium bowl, whisk together the beer, flour, paprika, and garlic. Let this mixture stand for 2 hours. Coat the avocado wedges with the beer batter. Deep-fry the avocado wedges in hot oil for about 3 minutes or until they are golden brown. Serve the avocado wedges with the salsa.

{ CHOCOLATE-DIPPED BANANAS }

· Yields 4 Servings

4	firm bananas, peeled, and cut into 3 pieces
2	cups beer batter (2 cups flour + 1 pint beer blended until smooth)
	Oil
	Juice from 2 lemons
½	cup honey
1	cup whipped cream (add a little sugar to enhance flavoring)
	Chocolate, melted

Coat the bananas with the beer batter. In a skillet, heat the oil to 350°. Add the bananas, cooking them until they are golden and crispy. Remove the bananas and sprinkle them with the lemon juice and honey. Top the bananas with the sweetened whipped cream and serve them with the dipping chocolate.

❧ CHOCOLATE-DIPPED STRAWBERRIES ❧

· Yields 8 Servings

1	ounce yeast
9	ounces beer
	Pinch of salt
	Pinch of sugar
1	teaspoon white wine vinegar
6	ounces all-purpose flour (plus extra for coating)
	Oil
1	pound strawberries, hulled and halved
	Powdered sugar
	Whipped cream
	Chocolate, melted

In a large bowl, dissolve the yeast in the beer. Add the salt, sugar, and vinegar, mixing well. Sift the 6 ounces of flour into the mixture. Beat the mixture until it is creamy. Refrigerate the mixture for 20 minutes. In a frying pan, heat the oil to 350°. Dip the strawberries into the extra flour. Coat the strawberries with the beer batter. Place the strawberries into the hot oil and fry them until they are golden. Drain the strawberries on paper towels and coat them with the powdered sugar. Serve the strawberries with the whipped cream and dipping chocolate.

"A FINE BEER MAY BE JUDGED WITH ONLY ONE SIP, BUT IT'S BETTER TO BE THOROUGHLY SURE."

Bohemian proverb

❊⟩ APPLE TREE RINGS ⟨❊

· Yields 4 Servings

¼	cup confectioners' sugar
½	teaspoon ground cinnamon
1⅓	cups all-purpose flour (plus extra for coating)
2	egg yolks, beaten
¾	cup flat beer
	Oil
2	egg whites
	Pinch of cream of tartar
	Pinch of salt
1	tablespoon sugar
2	large red apples, peeled, cored, and cut into ¼-inch rings

In a small bowl, combine the confectioners' sugar and cinnamon, mixing well. Set this mixture aside.

In a medium bowl, combine the flour and egg yolks. Stir in the beer. Refrigerate this mixture for 2 hours to overnight.

In a skillet, heat 1-inch of oil to 375°.

In another medium bowl, whip together the egg whites, cream of tartar, salt, and sugar until the mixture forms soft peaks. Fold this mixture into the beer mixture. Coat the apple rings with the extra flour. Coat the apple rings with the batter.

Fry the apple rings until they are crispy. Drain the apple rings on paper towels and dust them with the confectioners' sugar and cinnamon mixture.

CHAPTER 7

Sandwiches

❖{ 4TH OF JULY BURGERS }❖

· Yields 4 to 5 Burgers

1	pound ground beef
1	tablespoon butter
1	teaspoon beef bouillon
½	teaspoon Worcestershire sauce
2	tablespoons beer
	Seasoned salt to taste
	Garlic salt to taste
	Pepper to taste
1	onion, sliced
1	cup sliced mushrooms
2	to 3 slices cheese
	Hamburger buns

In a mixing bowl, break-up the ground beef and form it into 4 to 5 patties. In a frying pan, combine and sauté the butter, bouillon, Worcestershire sauce, beer, and seasonings for approximately 2 to 3 minutes until the mixture begins to turn brown.

Add the patties and reduce the heat to medium high. Drain the excess grease. Add the onions, mushrooms, pepper, and salts. Stir to coat the patties slightly with the pan juices. Fry the patties to desired completion, adding the cheese so that it melts on the patties.

Set the patties aside and wipe the frying pan with a paper towel, removing excess juices. Place the buns into the frying pan to warm.

Place the patties onto the buns and garnish as desired.

❊{ 4TH OF JULY HOTDOGS }❊

· Yields 8 Servings

1	teaspoon water
2	tablespoons beer
½	teaspoon beef bouillon
1	pound or 8 hotdogs
	Salt and pepper to taste
	Hotdog buns

In a heated frying pan, combine the water, beer, and bouillon. Add the hotdogs, continually turning them until the juice is absorbed or fried-off. Fry the hotdogs to desired doneness, seasoning to taste. Set the hotdogs aside and wipe the frying pan with a paper towel, removing excess juices. Place the buns into the frying pan to warm. Place the hotdogs onto the buns and garnish as desired.

"SOME PEOPLE WANTED CHAMPAGNE AND CAVIAR WHEN THEY SHOULD HAVE HAD BEER AND HOTDOGS."

Dwight D. Eisenhower, 34th U.S. President

❦ MEMORIAL DAY BURGERS ❦

· Yields 6 Servings

2	pounds ground beef
	Dash of pepper
1	teaspoon Tabasco sauce
1	clove garlic, crushed
1/3	cup chili sauce
1/2	1-ounce package dry onion soup mix
1/2	cup beer

Preheat the oven to 400°. In a medium bowl, combine the ground beef, pepper, Tabasco sauce, garlic, chili sauce, dry onion soup mix, and 1/4 cup of the beer, mixing well. Form the mixture into 6 patties. Bake the patties for about 10 minutes until they are browned. Baste the patties with the remaining beer. Continue baking the patties for about 10 minutes or until desired doneness.

"SOME GUY IS CLAIMING THAT A TONIC OF BEER AND URINE WILL IMPROVE YOUR GARDEN. COME ON, IF THAT WAS TRUE, WOULDN'T FRAT HOUSES BE LIKE TROPICAL RAIN FORESTS?"

Jay Leno, American comedian and TV host

❧ MEMORIAL DAY HOTDOGS ❧

· Yields 10 Servings

¼	cup (½ stick) butter
12	ounces beer
1	large onion, thinly sliced
1	pound hotdogs
10	hot dog buns

In a saucepan, melt the butter. Add the beer and onion. Cook the mixture, covered, over a low heat for 30 minutes. Transfer the saucepan to a grill. Heat the hotdogs on the grill. While the hotdogs are grilling, dip them into the beer sauce a few times. Continue to grill the hotdogs to desired doneness. Place the hotdogs on the hot dog buns and top them with the cooked onions and the remaining sauce as desired.

❧ MICROWAVABLE HOTDOGS ❧

· Yields 4 Servings

12	ounces beer
1	pound hotdogs
	Hot dog buns (warmed)
	Sauerkraut (warmed)

In a casserole dish, combine the beer and hotdogs. Heat the mixture, covered, in a microwave for 6 to 8 minutes until it is heated thoroughly. Serve the hotdogs on the buns and top them with the sauerkraut.

❖{ HUMMUS WRAP }❖

· Yields 1 Serving

3	tablespoons red pepper hummus
2	tablespoons beer
	Extra virgin olive oil
1	soft tortilla shell
	Garlic powder to taste
	Italian seasoning (any kind)
	Grated Parmesan cheese
1	fresh tomato, sliced
1	sweet onion, sliced to taste
	Goat or other cheese
	Pepperoni slices
	Chopped fresh basil

In a bowl, combine the hummus and beer. Spread the olive oil on the tortilla shell. Thinly spread the beer hummus mixture on the tortilla. Over the hummus, sprinkle the garlic powder, Italian seasoning, and grated Parmesan cheese. Place the tomatoes and onions over the mixture. Add the cheese. Sprinkle everything again with Italian seasoning and olive oil. Top the mixture with a few pepperoni slices and fresh basil. On foil, bake the wrap at 375° to 400° for about 8 to 10 minutes or until the tortilla is golden brown and the cheese is melted.

"THIRSTY DAYS HATH SEPTEMBER,
APRIL, JUNE AND NOVEMBER;
ALL THE REST ARE THIRSTY TOO
EXCEPT FOR HIM WHO HATH HOME BREW."

Author Unknown

❧ CHEESE STEAK SANDWICHES ❧

· Yields 2 Servings

2	pats (1 tablespoon, halved) butter
2	tablespoons beer
1	tablespoon beef bouillon
1/4	large onion, cut into strips or small pieces
1/2	large pepper, cut into strips or small pieces
6	large fresh mushrooms, sliced
1	pound chipped steak, thinly sliced
	Seasoned salt to taste
	Garlic to taste
	Seasoned pepper to taste
4	slices cheese of choice
	Buns

In a frying pan, melt the butter and add the beer and bouillon. Add the onions, peppers, and mushrooms. Fry the mixture until the ingredients are soft. Add the steak to the mixture. The juices should be absorbed into the meat and other ingredients. Season to taste. Melt the cheese on top of the steak servings. Heat the buns and then place the steak, onions, and peppers onto the buns.

"ALWAYS DO SOBER WHAT YOU SAID YOU'D DO DRUNK. THAT WILL TEACH YOU TO KEEP YOUR MOUTH SHUT."

Ernest Hemingway, American author

❧ FRENCH DIP SANDWICHES ❧

· Yields 6 Servings

1	pound beef roast, trimmed of fat
1	1-ounce package onion soup mix
12	ounces beer
	Rolls of choice

In a crock-pot, cover the beef roast with the onion soup mix. Pour the beer over the beef roast. Cook the beef roast on low for about 8 hours. Pull the beef roast apart to make the sandwiches. Reserve the juices. Serve the beef on the rolls and use the reserved juices for dipping.

❧ SLOPPY JOES ❧

· Yields 6 to 8 Servings

2	pounds hamburger
1	large onion, chopped
1	large green pepper, chopped
1/2	cup V-8 juice
1/2	cup beer
1	to 2 cups ketchup (as needed to taste)
2	teaspoons chili powder (or as needed to taste)
1	teaspoon beef bouillon
	Salt and pepper to taste
	Seasoned salt to taste

In an electric frying pan, brown the hamburger, onion, and pepper. After the hamburger is cooked through, add all of the other ingredients, stirring to mix well. Simmer the mixture until it is thick.

CHAPTER 8

Sauces & Dressings

❧ BLAZING HOT WING SAUCE ❧

· Yields 2¼ Cups

1	packet Good Seasons Italian Dressing (powder)
½	cup (1 stick) butter
2	cups Frank's Red Hot Cayenne Pepper Sauce
6	tablespoons beer

If preparing with chicken wings:

1	to 2 dozen chicken wings

In a bowl, combine all of the ingredients, mixing well. The sauce is ready to serve, either over chicken wings or as a dipping sauce for chicken tenders.

To prepare the sauce with chicken wings: In a pot, boil the 1 to 2 dozen chicken wings until they float. Place the chicken wings into a baking dish. Pour the Blazing Hot Wing Sauce over the wings. Bake the wings at 350° for 45 minutes or until desired crispiness.

"BUT THE GREATEST LOVE—THE LOVE ABOVE ALL LOVES, EVEN GREATER THAN THAT OF A MOTHER... IS THE TENDER, PASSIONATE, UNDYING LOVE, OF ONE BEER DRUNKEN SLOB FOR ANOTHER."

Irish love ballad

❧ SWEET MUSTARD ❧

· Yields 3 Cups

⅔	cup beer
1	cup dry mustard powder
¼	cup molasses
¼	teaspoon salt
⅛	teaspoon ground turmeric
½	cup minced dried peaches or apricots
1	tablespoon minced candied ginger

In a bowl, combine the beer and mustard powder. Set aside for 30 minutes. Stir in the remaining ingredients. Spoon the mustard into ¾-pint jars, cap, and refrigerate. If desired, can the mustard for longer preservation.

"THERE ARE TWO REASONS FOR DRINKING: ONE IS WHEN YOU ARE THIRSTY, TO CURE IT; THE OTHER, WHEN YOU ARE NOT THIRSTY, TO PREVENT IT."

Thomas Love Peacock, English satirist, *Melincourt*

❧ STOVE-HOT MUSTARD ❧

· Yields 2 Cups

5	tablespoons dry mustard
2	tablespoons cornstarch
12	ounces beer

In a saucepan, combine the mustard and cornstarch. Add 3 tablespoons of beer and stir until the mustard is dissolved. Put the saucepan over a medium heat, stirring in the rest of the beer. Cook, stirring constantly, for 5 minutes until the beer foams, the alcohol dissipates, and the sauce is hot. Serve hot.

❧ BEER MUSTARD ❧

· Yields ⅔ Cup

½	cup dry mustard
1	teaspoon sugar
4	tablespoons flat beer
2	tablespoons extra virgin olive oil

In a bowl, combine all of the ingredients until well-blended. Transfer the mixture into a ½-pint jar, cover tightly, and refrigerate.

❧ HONEY MUSTARD ❧

· Yields 4 Small Jars

½	cup mustard powder
1	cup beer
½	cup cider vinegar
½	teaspoon freshly ground white pepper
4	eggs, lightly beaten
2	tablespoons honey
	Salt to taste

In a stainless steel bowl, combine the mustard powder, beer, vinegar, and white pepper, mixing well. Set the mixture aside for 3 hours. Create a double broiler and set the mixture over a pan of simmering water. Stir in the eggs. Stir the mixture for about 5 minutes or until the mixture thickens. Stir in the honey. Add the salt to taste. Pack the Honey Mustard into small jars and refrigerate.

❧ TWO-MINUTE MUSTARD ❧

· Yields 2 Cups

1	cup mustard powder
¼	cup cold water
½	cup beer

In a medium bowl, whisk together the mustard powder and cold water. Set this mixture aside for approximately 10 minutes. Stir the beer into the mustard powder mixture, mixing well. Serve immediately or store in a jar in the refrigerator.

❧ PANCAKE SYRUP ❧

· Yields 1 Cup

½	cup light beer
1½	cups firmly packed brown sugar
½	teaspoon ground cinnamon
3	tablespoons butter

In a saucepan, combine all of the ingredients. Bring the mixture to a boil. Serve the syrup warm.

"WHY, WE'LL SMOKE AND DRINK OUR BEER.
FOR I LIKE A DROP OF GOOD BEER, I DOES.
I'ZE FOND OF GOOD BEER, I IS.
LET GENTLEMEN FINE SIT DOWN TO THEIR WINE.
BUT WE'LL ALL OF US HERE STICK TO OUR BEER."

Old Somersetshire English song

❖⦃ RAISIN SAUCE ⦄❖

· Yields 1½ Cups

¼	cup firmly packed brown sugar
1½	tablespoons cornstarch
⅛	teaspoon salt
1	cup beer
¼	cup raisins, halved
8	whole cloves
1	2-inch stick cinnamon
¼	lemon, diced
1	tablespoon butter

In a saucepan, combine the brown sugar, cornstarch, and salt. Stir in the beer and raisins. Place the cloves, cinnamon, and lemon into a cheesecloth bag. Suspend the bag in the sauce as it heats. Cook and stir the sauce for 10 minutes. Remove the spices in the bag. Add the butter to the sauce. Serve the sauce very hot with pork, ham, or another meat of choice.

"GIVE MY PEOPLE PLENTY OF BEER, GOOD BEER AND CHEAP BEER, AND YOU WILL HAVE NO REVOLUTION."

Queen Victoria, English monarch

❧ BARBECUE SAUCE ☙

· Yields 2 Cups

1	cup ketchup
1	cup beer
½	cup chopped onion
¼	cup vinegar
1	tablespoon Worcestershire sauce
1	tablespoon prepared mustard
⅛	teaspoon hot pepper sauce
½	teaspoon salt

In a saucepan, combine all of the ingredients and bring to a boil. Reduce heat. Simmer, uncovered, for 30 minutes. Serve warm.

"He that buys land buys many stones.
He that buys flesh buys many bones.
He that buys eggs buys many shells,
But he that buys good beer buys nothing else."

Author Unknown

❧ SPICY BARBECUE SAUCE ❧

· Yields 12 Servings

2	14-ounce bottles ketchup
1	12-ounce bottle chili sauce
½	cup mustard
1	teaspoon mustard powder
1	teaspoon salt
1½	cups firmly packed brown sugar
2	tablespoons pepper
1	5-ounce bottle steak sauce
½	cup Worcestershire sauce
1	tablespoon soy sauce
12	ounces beer
2	teaspoons minced garlic

In a saucepan, combine all of the ingredients, except the garlic, mixing well. Simmer the mixture, uncovered, over a medium heat for 30 minutes. Add the garlic right before using the sauce. Baste your meat of choice with the Spicy Barbecue Sauce during the last 15 minutes of grilling.

"BEER... A HIGH AND MIGHTY LIQUOR."

Julius Caesar, Roman military and political leader

❧ SAUCE FOR BAKED FISH ❧

· Yields 1 Serving

1	cup medium white sauce (2 tablespoons cornstarch + 1 cup water or milk)
1	cup shredded Cheddar cheese
2	teaspoons Worcestershire sauce
1	teaspoon paprika
1	teaspoon mustard
1	cup beer
1	tablespoon capers

In a saucepan, combine the white sauce, Cheddar cheese, Worcestershire sauce, paprika, and mustard, mixing well. Heat the mixture, constantly stirring, until the Cheddar cheese melts. Slowly add the beer. Add the capers, continuing to stir. Serve this sauce with baked fish.

❧ HOT SAUCE FOR FISH ❧

· Yields 1 Serving

1	cup mayonnaise
¼	cup hot sauce
¼	cup beer
1	tablespoon mustard
1	tablespoon lemon juice
1	teaspoon horseradish

In a medium bowl, combine all of the ingredients, mixing well. Serve with your favorite fish dish.

❖{ CHICKEN BASTING SAUCE }❖

· Yields 2 Cups

1½	cups beer
¼	cup any citrus or ginger marmalade
1	tablespoon dry mustard
1	tablespoon peeled and minced fresh ginger
2	cloves garlic, minced
¼	teaspoon salt
1	teaspoon sugar or honey

In a bowl, combine and whisk all of the ingredients together. Use immediately as a basting sauce for chicken.

❖{ BEER GLAZE FOR HAM }❖

· Yields 1½ Cups

1	cup firmly packed brown sugar
3	tablespoons mustard
½	cup beer

In a medium bowl, combine the brown sugar and mustard, mixing well until a paste forms. Slowly add the beer, mixing well. Using a part of the mixture, baste the ham before baking it. Throughout the baking process, brush the rest of the glaze on the ham.

❖❳ HORSERADISH SAUCE ❳❖

· Yields 1½ Cups

2	tablespoons butter
2	tablespoons all-purpose flour
1	cup light beer (cold)
2	tablespoons grated horseradish root
	Salt to taste
	Prepared sharp mustard to taste
	Pepper to taste
2	egg yolks
½	cup sweet cream

In a saucepan, melt the butter. Add and sauté the flour until medium brown. Gradually stir in the light beer, beating, so as to keep the sauce smooth. Simmer for 10 minutes. Add the horseradish root, salt, mustard, and pepper. Mix. Keep the sauce over a low heat. In a bowl, beat the egg yolks in the sweet cream. Slowly add ½ cup of the sauce to the egg yolk mixture. Blend and turn back into the rest of the sauce. Stir and heat, but do not boil.

"IF A LIAR AND DECEIVER COMES AND SAYS, 'I WILL PROPHESY FOR YOU PLENTY OF WINE AND BEER,' HE WOULD BE JUST THE PROPHET FOR THIS PEOPLE!"

Bible (Micah 2: 11)

❈❦ SPAGHETTI & PIZZA SAUCE ❦❈

· Yields 3 Quarts

2	garlic cloves, minced
1	medium sweet onion, chopped
2	tablespoons extra virgin olive oil
1	6-ounce can tomato paste
2	teaspoons chopped dry basil leaves (or 1 bunch fresh basil leaves)
2	tablespoons beer
3	28-ounce cans crushed tomatoes (or 2 cans crushed and 1 can sauce)
1	cup water
1	tablespoon sugar
1	teaspoon fresh oregano (or to taste)
	Salt and course black pepper to taste
2	tablespoons grated Parmesan and/or Romano cheese

In a pot, gently fry the garlic and onion in the olive oil until the mixture is golden brown. Add the tomato paste with the basil and sauté. Add the beer, tomatoes, water, sugar, oregano, salt, pepper, and cheese. Stir gently and simmer for at least five hours, stirring occasionally. If desired, add meatballs, chops, or steak cubes to the sauce.

"…SATISFY HIS SPIRIT WITH BEEF AND FOWL, BREAD AND BEER."

Inscription from an Egyptian tomb

❧ CHEESE SAUCE ❧

· Yields 4 Servings

½	cup shredded Monterey Jack cheese
½	cup shredded Cheddar cheese
1	teaspoon all-purpose flour
½	teaspoon mustard powder
½	teaspoon paprika
4	ounces beer
1	teaspoon hot sauce
¼	cup milk

In a medium bowl, combine the Monterey Jack cheese, Cheddar cheese, flour, mustard powder, and paprika, mixing well. In a saucepan over a low to medium heat, combine the beer and hot sauce. Gradually add the cheese mixture to the beer mixture, stirring continuously until the cheese melts. Add the milk, continuing to stir. Serve warm with pretzels, tortilla chips, or chicken.

"When the bee comes to your house, let her have beer; you may want to visit the bee's house some day."

Congoese Proverb

⁘⧘ COCKTAIL SAUCE ⧙⁘

· Yields 1¼ Cups

1	cup ketchup
2	tablespoons horseradish
1	teaspoon Worcestershire sauce
1	tablespoon beer

In a small bowl, combine all of the ingredients, mixing well. Serve chilled as a dipping sauce for shrimp and other seafood.

⁘⧘ MOLASSES SAUCE ⧙⁘

· Yields 3 Cups

1¼	cups chili sauce
¾	cup molasses (light and mild-flavored)
¾	cup beer
2	tablespoons Dijon mustard
1	tablespoon chili powder
2	teaspoons soy sauce
2	teaspoons Tabasco sauce
1½	teaspoons freshly squeezed lemon juice
1	teaspoon hickory-flavored liquid smoke

In a saucepan, combine all of the ingredients, mixing well. Bring the mixture to a boil over a medium heat while stirring. Reduce the heat and simmer the mixture, uncovered, until it thickens and is reduced to 2 cups. Continue to stir. Cool before using. Brush the Molasses Sauce on chicken, spareribs, or other meats of choice about 15 minutes before the end of the cooking time.

❧ PEANUT BUTTER SAUCE ❧

· Yields 6 to 8 Servings

1	teaspoon cracked black pepper
1	teaspoon garlic powder
½	teaspoon garlic salt
1	teaspoon crushed red pepper
½	teaspoon onion powder
½	teaspoon salt
½	teaspoon hot sauce
2	tablespoons Worcestershire sauce
1	18-ounce jar creamy peanut butter
24	ounces beer
2	cups milk

In a saucepan, combine all of the ingredients, except 12 ounces of the beer and the milk, mixing well. Bring the mixture to a boil over a medium-high heat. When the sauce thickens, turn the heat down to simmer the mixture. Add the other 12 ounces of the beer. Continue to simmer the mixture, uncovered, as the sauce thickens and slowly add the milk. Once the sauce is thick and thoroughly heated, use it to brush on your favorite meat, shish-kabobs, or vegetables.

"PROHIBITION MAKES YOU WANT TO CRY INTO YOUR BEER, AND DENIES YOU THE BEER TO CRY INTO."

Don Marquis, American journalist

·{ HERBED BUTTER }·

· Yields 1½ Cups

1	cup (2 sticks) butter (room temperature)
¼	teaspoon salt
2	tablespoons beer
1	teaspoon chervil
2	tablespoons minced chives
1	shallot, minced
1	teaspoon each: dried thyme, basil, and marjoram
1	small clove garlic, minced
¼	teaspoon finely ground pepper

In a medium bowl, cream the butter with the salt and beer. Blend in the remaining ingredients. Let the mixture stand at room temperature for 1 hour.

·{ BUTTER SAUCE }·

· Yields ¾ Cup

½	cup (1 stick) unsalted butter
½	cup beer
1	teaspoon garlic salt
1	teaspoon ground cayenne pepper
1	teaspoon ground mustard
1	tablespoon Worcestershire sauce

In a saucepan, melt the butter and start to simmer it. Gradually add the beer. Add the garlic salt, cayenne pepper, mustard, and Worcestershire sauce, mixing well. Boil the sauce for 2 minutes and then remove it from the heat. Use the sauce for steak, potatoes, or other foods of choice.

⚜ SPICY SALAD DRESSING ⚜

· Yields 5 Cups

1½	cups salad oil
1	cup beer
1	tablespoon Worcestershire sauce
2	10¾-ounce cans condensed tomato soup
1	small onion, grated
1	clove garlic, mashed
1	tablespoon sugar
2	tablespoons salt
1	tablespoon horseradish

In a medium bowl, combine all of the ingredients, mixing well. Chill the mixture until you are ready to serve it over greens. Mix again just before serving it.

"A LITTLE BIT OF BEER IS DIVINE MEDICINE."

Paracelsus, Swiss physician

CHAPTER 9

Marinades

❊{ BEEF MARINADE }❊

· Yields 8 Servings

24	ounces beer
2	teaspoons salt
½	cup olive oil
1	teaspoon ground cayenne pepper
1	tablespoon wine vinegar
1	tablespoon horseradish
1	teaspoon onion powder
2	tablespoons lemon juice
1	teaspoon garlic powder

In a medium bowl, combine all of the ingredients, mixing well. Use the Beef Marinade as a marinade or basting sauce.

❊{ SOUTHWESTERN MARINADE }❊

· Yields 4 Cups

2	cups red wine
12	ounces beer
1	small red onion, sliced
	Juice from 6 to 8 limes
¼	cup chopped fresh cilantro
½	teaspoon salt
¼	teaspoon pepper
¼	teaspoon red pepper flakes
¼	teaspoon ground cumin

In a medium bowl, combine all of the ingredients, mixing well. Use the marinade on your favorite meat.

❖{ BRISKET MARINADE }❖

· Yields 5 Cups

1	cup Worcestershire sauce
24	ounces beer
2	teaspoons vegetable oil
3	tablespoons lemon juice
1	teaspoon liquid smoke
1	cup soy sauce
1	teaspoon garlic powder (or to taste)
1	teaspoon hot sauce
1	tablespoon A-1 sauce
1	tablespoon apple cider vinegar

In a medium bowl, combine all of the ingredients, mixing well. Use the Brisket Marinade as a marinade or basting sauce.

"WE'RE WANTED MEN, WE'LL STRIKE AGAIN,
BUT FIRST LET'S HAVE A BEER."

Jimmy Buffett, American singer, "The Great Filling Station Holdup"

❊{ TUNA MARINADE }❊

· Yields 3 Cups

12	ounces beer
1	cup soy sauce
1/4	cup vegetable oil
2	tablespoons finely minced onion
2	tablespoons sugar
2	tablespoons vinegar
1	teaspoon mustard powder
1/2	teaspoon ground ginger
1/2	teaspoon ground cinnamon
	Juice from 2 limes

In a food processor, combine all of the ingredients, mixing well. Marinate the tuna for approximately 2 hours before cooking.

"When the beer bubbles, the masses forget their troubles."

The People's Daily, China

⁂{ RIB MARINADE }⁂

· Yields 7 Cups

4	cups beer
2	cups firmly packed brown sugar
1	cup cider vinegar
1	tablespoon chili powder
1	teaspoon ground cumin
1	teaspoon mustard powder
2	teaspoons hot red pepper flakes

In a saucepan, combine all of the ingredients, mixing well. Bring the mixture to a boil, remove it from the heat, and allow it to cool. Use the sauce to marinate ribs for at least 24 hours before grilling. Use any left-over Rib Marinade to baste the ribs while they are cooking.

⁂{ SPICY MARINADE }⁂

· Yields 3 Cups

1	cup beer
1	cup beef broth
1	teaspoon fresh thyme leaves
3	tomatoes, peeled, seeded, and diced
2	teaspoons Worcestershire sauce
1	teaspoon Tabasco sauce
2	bay leaves, crumbled
3/4	teaspoon cracked black peppercorns
1/4	cup chopped fresh parsley

In a medium bowl, combine all of the ingredients, mixing well. Use the marinade on your favorite meat of choice.

❖ BARBECUE MARINADE ❖

· Yields 10 Cups

2½	cups ketchup
9	ounces beer
¾	cup firmly packed brown sugar
¾	cup lemon juice
1½	cups chili sauce
½	cup mustard
1½	cups wine vinegar
1	tablespoon celery seed
1½	cups water
4	tablespoons Worcestershire sauce
2	tablespoons soy sauce
2	cloves garlic, minced
	Dash of hot sauce
	Ground pepper to taste

In a medium bowl, combine all of the ingredients, mixing well. Marinate your meat of choice overnight and use any reserved Barbecue Marinade for basting while cooking or grilling the meat.

"WHY SHOULD MOTHER GO WITHOUT HER NOURISHING GLASS OF ALE OR STOUT ON WASHING DAY?"

1920s anti-temperance slogan

CHAPTER 10

Beef

❧ GEORGIA BEEF ❧

· Yields 6 to 8 Servings

2	pounds stew beef, cut into 1-inch cubes
6	tablespoons butter
1	15-ounce can onions
1	13.25-ounce can mushrooms
1½	tablespoons all-purpose flour
1	tablespoon brown sugar
½	teaspoon salt
2	teaspoons mustard
4	peppercorns
1	bottle beer

In a skillet, sauté the beef in the butter until it is brown. Add the onions and mushrooms. Sprinkle the meat with the flour, brown sugar, and mustard. Add the peppercorns and beer. Place the meat in a casserole dish, cover, and cook at 275° for several hours or until desired doneness.

❧ GINGER BEEF ❧

· Yields 4 Servings

1	pound steak, cubed
1	medium onion, sliced
1	tablespoon butter
1	tablespoon oil
½	cup flat beer
1	teaspoon freshly ground ginger
1	tablespoon lemon juice
2	cups beef bouillon

In a Dutch oven, brown the steak and onion in the butter and oil. Add the beer, ginger, lemon juice, and bouillon. Cook, covered, for about 15 minutes, stirring constantly.

❊❳ GARLIC ROAST BEEF ❲❊

· Yields 10 to 12 Servings

1	4-pound beef top round roast
3/4	cup beer
2	tablespoons vegetable oil
2	cloves garlic, finely chopped
1/2	teaspoon salt
1/8	teaspoon pepper
2	teaspoons instant beef bouillon
1/4	cup water
2	tablespoons all-purpose flour

Pierce the beef roast thoroughly with a fork and place in a glass bowl. In a mixing bowl, combine the beer, vegetable oil, garlic, salt, and pepper. Pour the mixture over the beef. Cover and refrigerate the beef, turning it occasionally, for 1 hour.

Sprinkle the roast with the beef bouillon. In a casserole dish, place the beef fat side up on the rack. Reserve the marinade. Cook the roast at 325° for 1 1/2 to 2 hours for medium doneness. Use a meat thermometer to determine your preference of doneness. Cover the roast with foil and let stand for 15 minutes. The roast will continue to cook.

For the gravy, pour the drippings into another mixing bowl. Skim off the fat. Add the reserved marinade and enough water, if necessary, to make 1 cup. Shake the 1/4 cup of water and the flour in a tightly covered container. Stir gradually into the gravy.

❋⟩ BEEF STROGANOFF ⟨❋

· Yields 4 Servings

4	tablespoons butter
2	medium onions, sliced
1½	pounds sirloin steak, cut into ½-inch strips
4	medium carrots, scraped and cut into 1-inch chunks
8	ounces canned mushroom pieces, drained
1	to 2 teaspoons salt
½	teaspoon pepper
½	teaspoon grated nutmeg
¼	teaspoon caraway seed
1	tablespoon Worcestershire sauce
1	beef bouillon cube
12	ounces beer
1	cup sour cream
	Noodles (optional)

In a skillet, melt the butter. Sauté the onions for 5 minutes. When the onions are limp and translucent, lift them out of the skillet to a warm platter with a slotted spoon. Increase the heat under the skillet and quickly brown the meat. Return the onions to the skillet with the carrots, mushrooms, salt, pepper, nutmeg, caraway seed, and Worcestershire sauce. Stir the mixture well and then add the bouillon cube and beer. Cover and let simmer for about 20 minutes. Add the sour cream to the skillet. Heat the mixture through but do not boil. Serve alone or over noodles.

❖{ SPICY MEAT TURNOVERS }❖

· Yields 2 Servings

2	teaspoons butter
½	cup thinly sliced onion
1	cup beer, divided
¼	teaspoon salt
12	ounces lean ground beef
¾	cup water
1	teaspoon teriyaki sauce
1	teaspoon Dijon mustard
½	teaspoon browning sauce
1	tablespoon minced fresh parsley

In a skillet, melt the butter. Add the onion and sauté until softened. Add ½ cup of the beer. Cook until most of the liquid evaporates. Stir in the salt and set aside. Divide the beef into 2 equal balls.

On separate sheets of the wax paper, roll-out the balls, forming 2 6-inch flat circles. Place half of the onion mixture onto each circle. Fold over the circles, pressing the seams to form a half-moon effect. Remove the turnovers from the paper and broil them on a rack until they are browned on both sides, carefully turning them once with a spatula.

In the skillet, combine the water, teriyaki sauce, mustard, browning sauce, and remaining beer to create the sauce. Simmer until the sauce is slightly thickened. Add the turnovers and serve with the sauce. Sprinkle with the parsley.

⁖⧼ SOUTHWESTERN BRISKET ⧽⁖

· Yields 8 to 10 Servings

2	cloves garlic, minced
1/4	cup + 1 tablespoon firmly packed brown sugar
2	teaspoons ground cumin
1	teaspoon salt
1/2	teaspoon freshly ground pepper
1/4	teaspoon ground cinnamon
5	pounds beef brisket
2	large onions, wedged
1	cup beer
3	tablespoons tomato paste
2	dried chipotle chilies
8	to 10 small red potatoes, halved
8	ounces baby carrots

Preheat the oven to 325°. Line a casserole dish with foil, extending it about 3 inches beyond the sides.

In a small bowl, combine the garlic, 1 tablespoon of the brown sugar, cumin, salt, pepper, and cinnamon. Place the meat into the lined pan and rub the spice mixture all over the brisket. Scatter the onion over the meat.

In a medium bowl, combine the beer, tomato paste, and the remaining 1/4 cup of brown sugar. Pour this mixture over the meat and onions. Add the chilies. Cover with foil and crimp the edges tightly. Bake for 2 1/2 hours.

Remove the top layer of foil and spoon some of the pan juices over the meat. Bake for 1 more hour.

Remove from the oven and cool slightly. Using a slotted spoon, remove the onions and place them on top of the meat. Cover and refrigerate overnight.

Scrape the fat off of the juices and add the potatoes and carrots to the pan. Bake, uncovered, in a 350° oven for 1 to 1 1/2 hours.

⚜{ BEEF PYRAMIDS }⚜

· Yields 6 Servings

3½	pounds lean boneless beef rump or round (about 2 inches thick)
	Pinch of salt and pepper
	Flour
2	tablespoons butter
2	large onions, thinly sliced
2	large red peppers, halved
12	fresh mushrooms, coarsely chopped
1½	cups light beer
1½	tablespoons ketchup
1	tablespoon prepared mustard

Trim all the fat off of the meat. Slice the meat lengthwise into two strips about 3-inches wide. Cut a diagonal slice off one end of the strip. Starting at the point, cut diagonally in the opposite direction to make thick triangular pieces. Continue cutting until the roast is cut into triangles or pyramids. Sprinkle each piece of meat with salt and pepper, and dredge in the flour on all sides. In a skillet, melt the butter and brown the meat lightly, turning it carefully to maintain the pyramid shapes. Add the onions, peppers, and mushrooms to the skillet and brown lightly. Pour the light beer over the mixture. Stir in the ketchup and mustard. Cover tightly and simmer slowly for 1 to 1½ hours or until the meat is tender. If more sauce is desired, add another ¾ cup of light beer during cooking.

❖{ COUNTY FAIR CORN DOGS }❖

· Yields 10 Servings

⅔	cup freshly ground cornmeal (medium grind)
⅓	cup all-purpose flour (plus extra)
1	tablespoon salt
⅛	tablespoon cayenne pepper
1	egg, beaten
2	tablespoons olive oil
½	cup beer
10	hot dogs
10	wooden skewers
	Dijon mustard or mustard of choice for a dipping sauce

In a large bowl, combine the cornmeal, flour, salt, and cayenne pepper, mixing well.

In a small bowl, combine the egg, olive oil, and beer, mixing well. Add the egg mixture to the cornmeal mixture, blending well.

Place each hot dog on a skewer. Roll the hotdogs in the additional flour and then roll them in the batter. Fry the hotdogs, a few at a time, in hot oil, turning them to brown on all sides. Drain the hotdogs on paper towels. Use the mustard as a dipping sauce.

"HE WAS A WISE MAN WHO INVENTED BEER."
Plato, Greek philosopher

❊{ POT ROAST }❊

· Yields 6 to 8 Servings

4	pound chuck roast
1	yellow onion, sliced
2	ribs celery, chopped
1/4	cup chopped green peppers
1/3	cup water
1/2	cup chili sauce
1/4	teaspoon pepper
1/2	teaspoon salt
12	ounces beer (room temperature)

Place the roast in a large oven-proof pan with a lid. In a medium bowl, combine the rest of the ingredients, except the beer, mixing well. Pour this mixture over the roast. Cook the roast, uncovered, at 350° for 1 hour. Pour the beer over the roast and cook it, covered, for approximately 2 to 3 more hours until desired doneness.

"Back and side go bare, go bare,
Both foot and hand go cold;
But, belly, God send thee good ale enough,
Whether it be new or old."

from *Gammer Gurton's Needle,* Author Unknown

❊} CORNED BEEF & CABBAGE {❊

· Yields 8 Servings

4	pound corned beef brisket
12	ounces beer
1	small onion, peeled
1	bay leaf
½	teaspoon whole cloves
4	black peppercorns
2	ribs celery with the leaves
8	potatoes, peeled and halved
8	large carrots, peeled and halved
1	medium head green cabbage, quartered

In a kettle, cover the brisket with water. Add the beer, onion, bay leaf, cloves, peppercorns, and celery. Cover the kettle. Bring the mixture to a boil, reduce the heat, and simmer the mixture, covered, for 4 hours until the meat is tender. 30 minutes before the meat is done, remove the onion and celery. Skim the fat from the liquid. Add the potatoes and carrots and simmer the mixture, covered, for 15 minutes. Add the cabbage and simmer the mixture, covered, for 15 minutes. Remove the bay leaf before serving.

"MY PEOPLE MUST DRINK BEER."

Frederick the Great, King of Prussia

❧ TENDERLOINS ❧

· Yields 6 Servings

6	tenderloin fillets
	Salt and pepper to taste
1	tablespoon All-Purpose Seasoning
2	tablespoons safflower oil
4	strips bacon, chopped
2	tablespoons chopped chives
2	tablespoons chopped green onions
12	ounces beer
1	10-ounce can beef broth
1	tablespoon meat and poultry seasoning
3	ounces (6 tablespoons) butter, whipped
	Starch and water (to thicken sauce if needed)

Season the tenderloins with the salt, pepper, and All-Purpose Seasoning. In a skillet, combine the tenderloins and safflower oil, sautéing the tenderloins until they are brown on all sides. Remove the tenderloins and set them aside. In the same skillet, fry the bacon until it is crisp. Add the chives, green onions, beer, broth, salt, pepper, and meat and poultry seasoning, and simmer the mixture, covered, for 5 minutes. Blend in the butter and reduce the juices to half over a medium heat. Place the tenderloins in the sauce and cook them, covered, slowly at 275° until desired doneness.

❋❴ VEAL BRISKETS ❵❋

· Yields 6 to 8 Serves

2	jumbo Spanish onions, thinly sliced
2	medium parsnips, scrubbed and thinly sliced
2	veal briskets (5 pounds total)
	Kosher salt
	Freshly ground pepper
1	teaspoon paprika
1	teaspoon garlic powder
1	teaspoon dried thyme
12	ounces spicy chili sauce
1	cup beer
2	bay leaves

Preheat the oven to 325°. In a roasting pan, combine half of the onions and all of the parsnips. Place the briskets, fat side up, on the onions. Rub the briskets evenly with the salt, pepper, paprika, garlic powder, and thyme. Scatter the remaining onions over the briskets. Pour the chili sauce and beer over the briskets. Place a bay leaf on each brisket. Roast the briskets, covered, for about 2½ hours, basting occasionally, until the meat is tender. Remove the roasting pan from the oven and place the briskets on a large platter to cool. Discard the bay leaves, wrap the briskets in foil, and refrigerate. In a food processor, combine the onions and parsnips, puréeing well. Combine this mixture with the remaining gravy and pour it into a container. Cover and chill the mixture for 5 to 24 hours. Thinly slice the veal briskets across the grain. Preheat the oven to 325°. Combine the briskets and gravy in a roasting pan. Bake, covered, for 1 hour.

⁂{ VEAL MEATBALLS }⁂

· Yields 4 Servings

2	slices white bread, crusts removed
1	cup beer
4	tablespoons butter
1	small onion, chopped
1	clove garlic, crushed
1¼	pounds ground veal
1	egg, lightly beaten
	Salt and pepper to taste
	Grated nutmeg to taste
1	tablespoon fresh lemon juice
1	teaspoon sugar
1	tablespoon chopped fresh parsley

In a small bowl, soak the bread in ¼ cup of the beer, then squeeze the bread dry. In a skillet, combine 2 tablespoons of the butter, onion, and garlic, sautéing the onion until it is transparent. In a medium bowl, combine the veal with the soaked bread, onion, garlic, egg, salt, pepper, and nutmeg. Shape the mixture into meatballs. In the skillet with the remaining butter, cook the meatballs until they are browned. Pour in the rest of the beer and lemon juice. Add the sugar. Simmer the mixture, covered, for 30 minutes. Using a slotted spoon, transfer the meatballs to a heated platter. Reduce the sauce by a one-fourth over a high heat. Pour the sauce through a sieve over the meatballs and sprinkle them with the parsley.

⁖⟩ LIME SHORT RIBS ⟨⁖

· Yields 4 to 6 Servings

4	pounds country-style beef short ribs
1	cup beer
½	cup lime juice

Place the ribs into a casserole dish. In a bowl, combine the beer and lime juice. Pour this marinade over the ribs. Refrigerate, covered, overnight, turning occasionally. Bring the ribs to room temperature 2 hours before cooking. Prepare the grill. Remove the ribs from the marinade and place them on 2 sheets of foil, each large enough to make 2 packets to wrap and seal the ribs. Sprinkle 2 tablespoons of the marinade on the ribs and seal the packets. Set aside the remaining marinade. Place the rib packets onto the grill. Cook, covered, for 1 to 1½ hours until the ribs are tender. Remove the ribs from the foil, drain, and place back on the grill. Baste once with the reserved marinade and grill for 15 to 20 minutes over medium coals until crisp.

"BLESSED IS THE MOTHER WHO GIVES BIRTH TO A BREWER."

Czech saying

CHAPTER 11

Poultry & Eggs

❖} DRUNKEN CHICKEN {❖

· Yields 4 Servings

2½	to 3 pounds chicken
4	tablespoons butter
	Salt and pepper to taste
1	tablespoon chopped shallots
½	cup gin
1	cup heavy cream
2½	cups diced fresh mushrooms
2	cups beer
	Cayenne pepper
2	tablespoons chopped fresh parsley

Truss the chicken. In a casserole dish over a moderate heat, melt 2 tablespoons of the butter. Turn the chicken in the butter until it is golden. Add salt and pepper to taste, cover, and cook for 30 minutes at a medium heat. Remove the chicken to a heated dish and keep it covered in a warm place. In the same casserole dish, cook the shallots at a medium heat. When the shallots are golden, put the chicken back into the casserole, pour on the gin, and flame it. Add 1 tablespoon of the butter, 2 tablespoons of the cream, and the mushrooms. Pour in the beer and season with the salt, pepper, and a little cayenne pepper. Cover and simmer for 15 minutes.

When the chicken is well-cooked, put it on a chopping board and cut it into 4 pieces. Place the chicken on a serving dish and keep it warm and covered.

Pour the rest of the cream into the casserole dish and boil it vigorously for several minutes to thicken the liquid. Remove the casserole from the heat and add the rest of the butter. Let the butter melt. Pour the sauce over the chicken. Garnish with the parsley.

❧ GRILLED HERB CHICKEN ❧

· Yields 4 to 6 Servings

1	tablespoon minced garlic
1	teaspoon kosher salt
¼	teaspoon white pepper
¼	teaspoon cayenne pepper
1	teaspoon paprika
1	teaspoon coriander
2	tablespoons chopped basil
2	tablespoons chopped thyme
2	tablespoons chopped marjoram
2	teaspoons coarsely ground pepper
1	2- to 3-pound whole chicken, washed and dried
1	cup chopped fresh herbs of choice
2	tablespoons olive oil
12	ounces beer

In a medium bowl, combine the garlic, kosher salt, white pepper, cayenne pepper, paprika, coriander, basil, thyme, marjoram, and pepper, mixing well. Using this mixture, thoroughly rub the chicken inside and out. Place the fresh herbs inside the chicken's hollowed cavity. Brush the chicken with the olive oil. Place the chicken in an ovenproof dish. Pour the beer over the chicken. Grill the chicken, covered, over hot charcoals for 1½ hours, basting the chicken with more beer every 15 to 20 minutes.

❊❴ PRETZEL CHICKEN ❵❊

· Yields 4 Servings

⅓	cup all-purpose flour
1	teaspoon paprika
2	teaspoons salt
¼	teaspoon ground ginger
¼	teaspoon pepper
½	cup beer
1	egg
½	cup crushed pretzels
¼	cup grated Parmesan cheese
¼	cup crushed bacon bits
1	tablespoon dried parsley flakes
1	whole chicken, cut-up

In a medium bowl, combine the flour, paprika, salt, ginger, and pepper, mixing well. Add the beer and egg, beating the mixture until it forms a smooth batter.

In a plastic bag, combine the pretzels, Parmesan cheese, bacon, and parsley, shaking to mix well. Dip the chicken pieces into the batter, coating them completely. Place the chicken pieces in the plastic bag and shake the bag to coat the chicken with the pretzel mixture. Place the chicken in a shallow baking dish. Bake the chicken, covered, at 350° for 30 minutes.

Remove the cover and continue baking for approximately 30 minutes or until desired doneness.

⁂} Chicken with Shiitake Mushrooms {⁂

· Yields 6 Servings

2	large shallots, peeled and sliced
1	tablespoon extra virgin olive oil
6	6-ounce skinless, boneless chicken breasts
	Flour (for coating)
2	tablespoons extra virgin olive oil
4	ounces shiitaki mushrooms, sliced
1½	cups beef broth
1	teaspoon chopped fresh sage
¼	cup butter (room temperature)
⅓	cup all-purpose flour
1	cup beer
¼	cup sour cream
	Salt and pepper to taste
2	tablespoons diced roasted pepper

Place the shallots and the 1 tablespoon of olive oil into a small skillet over a low heat. Sauté slowly for about 25 minutes until the shallots are lightly browned and caramelized. Coat the chicken lightly with flour. Sauté the coated chicken in the 2 tablespoons of olive oil in a large skillet until the chicken is half done and lightly browned on both sides. Remove the chicken to a baking pan. Bake in a 375° oven for 10 to 12 minutes or until done, but still tender and juicy.

In a large skillet, sauté the mushrooms for 30 to 40 seconds. Add the shallots, broth, and sage. Bring the broth mixture to a slow simmer.

In a bowl, mix the butter and the ⅓ cup of the flour. Add a little at a time to the broth, stirring vigorously to prevent lumps. Reduce the heat and cook for 7 or 8 more minutes. Slowly add the beer, tasting as you go. It is not necessary to add it all. Add the sour cream and adjust the seasoning with the salt and pepper to taste. Add the roasted pepper. Pour the broth over the chicken.

❊❴ FRIED CHICKEN ❵❊

· Yields 6 Servings

1	3-pound broiler-fryer chicken, skinned, rinsed, and cut up
	Lightly salted water
1	cup biscuit mix
½	teaspoon onion salt
¼	teaspoon garlic powder
¼	to ½ teaspoon ground red pepper
1	egg, beaten
½	cup beer
	Oil for deep frying

In a saucepan, cover the chicken with the lightly salted water. Bring the water to a boil and reduce the heat. Cover and simmer for 20 minutes. Drain the water and pat the chicken dry with paper towels.

In one bowl, combine the biscuit mix, onion salt, garlic powder, and red pepper. In another bowl, combine the egg and beer. Add this mixture to the biscuit mixture. Beat the combined mixtures until they are one smooth mixture.

In a deep fryer, heat the oil to 365°. Dip the chicken pieces, one at a time, into the beer batter, gently shaking off the excess batter. Fry the chicken in the hot oil, two or three pieces at a time, for 2 or 3 minutes or until golden, turning them once. Drain well.

❊{ CHICKEN FINGERS }❊

· Yields 4 Servings

1	large egg
3/4	cup beer
1	cup all-purpose flour
1	teaspoon baking soda
1	teaspoon salt
	Freshly ground pepper to taste
1 1/4	cups vegetable oil
3	chicken halves, skinless, boneless, and cut into strips

In a medium bowl, lightly beat the egg with a whisk. Beat in the beer. Beat in the flour, baking soda, salt, and pepper, whisking until the batter is smooth. Cover the batter and let it stand for 30 minutes.

In a skillet, heat the vegetable oil until it reaches 360°. A deep fryer can also be used. Dip the chicken strips into the beer batter, coating them completely. Lower each chicken strip into the hot oil, turning the chicken strips until they are golden. This should take approximately 5 minutes. Drain the chicken strips on paper towels.

Serve the chicken strips with Ranch dressing, blue cheese dressing, or the Blazing Hot Wing Sauce on page 118.

"A PLEASANT APERTIF, AS WELL AS A GOOD CHASER FOR A SHORT QUICK WHISKEY, AS WELL AGAIN FOR A FINE SUPPER DRINK, IS BEER."

M.F.K. Fisher, American author

❋⟩ SCRAMBLED EGGS ⟨❋

· Yields 2 Servings

6	eggs
	Seasoned salt to taste
¼	cup water
1	tablespoon butter
2	tablespoons beer
1	teaspoon chicken bouillon
	Pepper to taste

In a bowl, combine the eggs, seasoned salt, and water. In a frying pan, melt the butter. Add the beer, bouillon, and pepper. Simmer the mixture for approximately 2 minutes until it is brown. Add the egg mixture to the frying pan and scramble the eggs to desired doneness. For fine scrambled eggs, continually chop the egg mixture with a spatula while frying it. For thicker scrambled eggs, flip the egg mixture over with a spatula while frying it.

❋⟩ BREAKFAST OMELET ⟨❋

· Yields 1 Serving

2	to 3 eggs
¼	cup water
2	to 3 tablespoons beer
	Seasoned salt to taste
¾	cup chopped spinach
	Onions to taste, chopped
	Red or yellow peppers to taste, chopped
⅓	cup sliced mushrooms
	Butter

In a bowl, whisk the eggs, water, beer, and seasoned salt together. Add the spinach, onions, peppers, and mushrooms. Stir well. In a frying pan, melt enough butter to coat the bottom. Once the coating of butter is bubbling, add the egg mixture. Using a spatula, gentle flop the egg mixture over until it's firm. Fold the flattened egg mixture in half and serve warm.

❖{ CHICKEN WINGS CASSEROLE }❖

· Yields 4 Servings

2	teaspoons butter
2	teaspoons vegetable oil
40	chicken wings
1/2	teaspoon salt
1/4	teaspoon pepper
1	onion, chopped
1	clove garlic, minced
1	tomato, peeled, seeded, and chopped
1	green pepper, chopped
1/4	cup beer
1/2	cup chicken stock

Preheat the oven to 350°. In a large skillet, combine the butter and vegetable oil, melting the butter over a medium heat. Add the chicken wings, seasoning them with the salt and pepper. Brown the chicken wings on all sides for 6 to 8 minutes. Remove the chicken wings and place them in a casserole dish.

In the skillet, combine the onion, garlic, tomato, and green pepper, stirring and sautéing the mixture for 2 to 3 minutes or until the onions are limp. Stir in the beer and chicken stock. Pour this mixture over the chicken wings in the casserole dish. Bake the chicken wings, uncovered, for 25 minutes or until desired doneness.

❧ MICROWAVABLE BARBECUED TURKEY DRUMSTICKS ❧

· Yields 6 Servings

1	package frozen or fresh turkey drumsticks, defrosted
1	cup barbecue sauce
½	cup beer
¼	teaspoon salt
⅛	teaspoon pepper

In a casserole dish, arrange the turkey drumsticks. In a bowl, combine the barbecue sauce, beer, salt, and pepper. Pour the mixture over the turkey. Cover the casserole tightly and microwave on high for 10 minutes.

Turn the drumsticks over. Cover the casserole tightly and microwave on medium for 25 minutes.

Turn the drumsticks again. Cover and microwave for 25 to 40 minutes until the meat feels very soft when pressed between the fingers. Place the drumsticks on a platter to serve.

"THE MOUTH OF A PERFECTLY HAPPY MAN IS FILLED WITH BEER."

Ancient Egyptian saying

CHAPTER 12

Pork

❦ BRAISED PORK WITH GRAVY ❦

· Yields 4 to 6 Servings

2	teaspoons finely minced garlic
1	tablespoon soy sauce
2	tablespoons firmly packed brown sugar
1/4	teaspoon ground allspice
1/4	teaspoon ground cayenne pepper
1/2	teaspoon salt
4	to 4 1/2 pounds (trimmed weight) picnic shoulder, rind removed
2 1/2	cups beer
2	bay leaves
6	cups tightly packed sliced onions
2	tablespoons cornstarch (dissolved in 3 tablespoons water)

In a bowl, make a paste by mashing together the garlic, soy sauce, brown sugar, allspice, cayenne pepper, and salt. Rub the mixture into the picnic shoulder. Pour the beer into a cooker and add the bay leaves. Set the rack in place. Place half of the onions on the rack and set the pork on top. Spread the remaining onions over the pork. Lock the lid in place and over a high heat, bring to a high pressure. Adjust the heat to maintain the high pressure. Cook for 55 minutes.

Let the pressure drop naturally or use a quick-release method. Remove the lid, tilting it away from you to allow any excess steam to escape. Check the pork with a meat thermometer inserted into the center. It should register 170°. If not, lock the lid back in place and return the pork to high pressure for a few more minutes.

Remove the pork to a platter and set aside in a warm place. Remove the rack. If there is more than 2 cups of sauce, boil vigorously over a high heat to reduce. Whisk in just enough of the cornstarch solution to thicken the gravy while cooking at a low boil for 2 to 3 minutes. Serve the gravy with the pork.

⁘⟩ PORK LOIN ⟨⁘

· Yields 6 Servings

2	pounds pork loin
1	teaspoon salt
¼	teaspoon freshly ground pepper
1	large onion, thinly sliced
1	tablespoon shortening
1	tablespoon sugar
1	cup beer
¾	cup water

In a casserole dish, sprinkle the pork loin with the salt and pepper. Let stand.

In one saucepan, cook the onion in the shortening until it is transparent, but not brown. Remove the onion. Brown the pork in the shortening. Place the onions back into the pan with the pork.

In another saucepan, dissolve the sugar in the beer and add it to the pork. Simmer the mixture until the beer takes on a golden-brown color. Add the water. Simmer for 20 minutes and add more water if necessary. Simmer for a few more minutes until the meat is tender.

"In wine there is wisdom. In beer there is strength. In water there is bacteria."

German saying

❧ SOAKED PORK LOIN ❧

· Yields 4 to 6 Servings

12	ounces beer
1/2	cup dark corn syrup
1/2	cup finely chopped onion
1/3	cup mustard
1/4	cup vegetable oil
1	to 2 tablespoons chili powder (or to taste)
2	cloves garlic, minced
3	pounds boneless pork loin

In a medium bowl, combine all of the ingredients, except the pork loin, mixing well. Place the pork in a casserole dish and pour the mixture over it. Cover and refrigerate the pork overnight, occasionally turning it. Remove the pork from the marinade, reserving the marinade. Grill the pork, basting it frequently with the reserved marinade, for approximately 1 to 1½ hours once a meat thermometer reads 155°.

❧ SIMPLE GRILLED PORK ❧

· Yields 4 Servings

1	pork loin
1	small bottle beer
	Lemon pepper seasoning to taste

Marinate the pork in the beer overnight. Rub the lemon pepper seasoning on all sides of the pork. Grill the pork until desired doneness.

❊{ PORK ROAST }❊

· Yields 6 Servings

1	very large onion, coarsely chopped
2	cloves garlic, minced
2	pounds boneless pork loin
1/2	teaspoon salt
1/4	teaspoon white pepper
1/2	teaspoon paprika
1 1/2	cups chicken broth
1 1/4	cups beer
3	tablespoons all-purpose flour
1/4	cup cold water

Preheat the oven to 325°. In a skillet, arrange the onions. Rub the garlic on the pork. Place on top of the onions. Sprinkle the roast with the salt, white pepper, and paprika. Pour the broth over the pork, just covering the onions. Roast the pork for 30 minutes, uncovered.

Pour the beer over the pork and continue to roast for 45 more minutes, until the meat thermometer registers 160°. Place the pork on a warm plate and cover.

In a bowl, combine the flour and water. Pour the flour mixture into the juice-onion mixture in the skillet. Cook the mixture over a high heat until the mixture boils and thickens. Simmer for 5 minutes and pour over the pork.

❊⟨ FRUITY PORK ROAST ⟩❊

· Yields 8 Servings

8	pitted dried prunes
12	ounces beer
½	teaspoon ginger
1	medium apple, peeled and chopped
1	teaspoon lemon juice
3	pounds boneless rolled pork loin roast, butterflied
	Salt and pepper to taste

In a saucepan, combine the prunes, beer, and ginger, heating the mixture to a boil. Remove the mixture from the heat and let it stand for 5 minutes.

In a small bowl, combine the apple chunks and lemon juice. This will prevent the apple chunks from browning. Drain the prunes, reserving the juice. Pat the prunes dry with paper towels. Add the prunes to the apple chunks, mixing well. Stuff the prune and apple mixture into the pork. Tie the pork with string to secure the fruit stuffing. Place the pork on a rack in a roasting pan. Roast the pork, covered, at 350° for approximately 2½ hours, allowing about 40 minutes per pound.

Periodically baste the pork with the reserved juice and season with the salt and pepper to taste. Place the finished pork on a heated platter. Create a gravy sauce from the remaining juices or serve with another sauce of choice.

❧ HONEY PORK ❧

· Yields 6 Servings

12	ounces stale beer
6	cloves garlic, minced
½	cup honey
½	cup Dijon mustard
	Salt and pepper to taste
¼	cup olive oil
4	tablespoons rosemary
3	pounds pork loin

In a blender, combine all of the ingredients, except the pork, blending well. Pierce the pork with a fork on all sides and place it in a zip-lock bag. Add the marinade to the pork in the bag. Chill the pork for approximately 12 hours to overnight, turning frequently.

Remove the pork from the bag and grill it, covered, for approximately 1½ hours or until desired doneness.

"FROM MAN'S SWEAT AND GOD'S LOVE, BEER CAME INTO THE WORLD."

Saint Arnold (aka Arnulf) of Metz, The Patron Saint of Brewers

❧ SOUTH OF THE BORDER PORK ❧

· Yields 8 Servings

2	small onions, chopped
2	carrots, peeled and sliced
5	pounds pork roast or loin
2	teaspoons salt
	Garlic to taste
½	teaspoon oregano (fresh or dried)
½	teaspoon ground coriander
¾	cup beer
	Olive oil
1	small onion, chopped
1	clove garlic, peeled and chopped
10	ounces tomatillos
½	teaspoon crumbled dried oregano
½	teaspoon dried cilantro
2	tablespoons wine vinegar
	Salt and pepper to taste

In a roasting pan, combine the 2 small onions and carrots. Rub the pork with the salt, garlic to taste, the ½ teaspoon of oregano, and coriander. Place the pork on top of the vegetables in the roasting pan. Add the beer. Roast the pork, covered, at 350° for 2¾ hours. Remove the pork, slice it, and place it on a heated platter.

In a skillet, combine the olive oil, the 1 small onion, and the 1 clove of garlic, sautéing the onion and garlic until they are limp. Drain the tomatillos, reserving the juice. In a blender, combine the tomatillos, ½ cup of the reserved juice, the sautéed onion and garlic, olive oil to taste, the ½ teaspoon of dried oregano, and cilantro, puréeing well. Heat the skillet over a moderate heat and pour in the tomatillos sauce, cooking it, uncovered, for 10 minutes. Remove the sauce from the heat and add the wine vinegar, salt, and pepper, mixing well. Chill the sauce and serve it with the pork.

❖{ SWEET 'N' TANGY PORK SAUTÉ }❖

· Yields 4 Servings

8	ounces beer
1	tablespoon Dijon mustard
1½	teaspoons orange peel
1	teaspoon salt
¼	teaspoon Worcestershire sauce
1	clove garlic, minced
1	pound cooked pork, julienne-cut into ¼-inch thick strips
1	tablespoon + 1 teaspoon vegetable oil
½	cup chopped onion
½	medium green bell pepper, cut into 1-inch squares
½	medium red bell pepper, cut into 1-inch squares
1	tablespoon + 1 teaspoon cornstarch + 1 tablespoon water
½	cup canned pineapple chunks (no sugar added)
8	canned apricot halves with ¼ cup juice (no sugar added)
2	cups cooked enriched rice (hot)

In a bowl, combine the beer, mustard, orange peel, salt, Worcestershire sauce, and garlic. Add the pork. Cover and let marinate in the refrigerator for 30 minutes, turning occasionally.

In a skillet, heat the oil. Add the onion, green peppers, and red peppers. Sauté until the onion is translucent. Add the pork and marinade. Bring to a boil. Add the dissolved cornstarch and cook, stirring constantly, until the mixture thickens. Stir in the pineapple and apricots and heat. Serve with the rice.

⋅{ PORK CHOPS }⋅

⋅ Yields 4 Servings

4	pork chops
1/2	teaspoon salt
1/4	teaspoon pepper
1 1/2	tablespoons unbleached flour
1 1/2	tablespoons vegetable oil
4	small onions, thinly sliced
1/2	cup beer
1/2	cup beef broth (hot)
1	teaspoon cornstarch
	Cold water

Season the pork chops with the salt and pepper. Coat the pork chops with the flour. In a skillet, heat the vegetable oil. Add the pork chops, frying them for 3 minutes on each side. Add the onions and cook the pork chops for 5 minutes, turning them once. Pour in the beer and broth. Simmer the mixture, covered, for 15 minutes.

Remove the pork chops to a heated platter. Season the pork chops to taste.

In a small bowl, combine the cornstarch with a little cold water, blending well. Stir this mixture into the sauce in the frying pan. Cook the sauce, uncovered, until it is thick and bubbling. Pour the sauce over the pork chops.

❧ PORK LOAF ❧

· Yields 4 Servings

2	pounds lean pork
1	pound smoked ham hocks
1½	cups dry bread crumbs
2	eggs, beaten
1	teaspoon salt
¼	teaspoon white pepper
	Beer

Have your butcher grind the pork and ham hocks together. In a medium bowl, combine the meat mixture, bread crumbs, eggs, salt, and white pepper, mixing well. Form the mixture into a loaf. Roll the loaf in a cheesecloth and tie the ends securely. Place the loaf in a pot and cover it with beer. Simmer the loaf, covered, slowly for 2¼ hours.

Serve the loaf sliced on bread or alone with a salad.

"IT TAKES BEER TO MAKE THIRST WORTH-WHILE."

German saying

❧ HAM ❧

· Yields 6 to 8 Servings

20	whole cloves
1	5 or 6 pound ham
12	ounces beer

Press the cloves into the surface of the ham. Place in a roaster, and pour the beer over the ham. Bake the ham at 350° for 3 hours. Remove the cloves and serve.

❧ BACON ❧

· Yields 3 to 4 Servings

3	ounces beer
1	pound bacon, diced into ½-inch pieces or strips

Put the beer and bacon into a frying pan. Cover and fry the bacon until it is almost done. Drain all excess grease and juices from the frying pan. Remove the cover and continue to fry the bacon until it is crispy.

⊰ GRILLED BRATWURST ⊱

· Yields 4 to 8 Servings

2	tablespoons butter
4	medium yellow onions, sliced
8	bratwurst links
24	ounces beer
	Hotdog buns
	Mustard

In a skillet, combine the butter and onions, sautéing the onions until they are tender. Place the bratwurst links on top of the onions and pour the beer over them. Simmer the bratwurst links, covered, for 15 minutes, turning them occasionally. Remove the bratwurst links from the skillet and keep them warm.

Over a high heat, cook the beer and onions, stirring often, until the cooking liquid is greatly reduced and the mixture reaches a spreadable consistency. Spoon the onion sauce into a small serving dish and set it aside, keeping it warm.

Place the bratwurst links on a heated grill, turning them often, until they are browned and crisp. Serve the bratwurst links on the hotdog buns along with the onion sauce, mustard, and any other toppings of choice.

"BEER, IF DRANK WITH MODERATION, SOFTENS THE TEMPER, CHEERS THE SPIRIT, AND PROMOTES HEALTH."

Thomas Jefferson, 3rd U.S. President

❈⟩ HONEY BARBECUED SPARERIBS ⟨❈

· Yields 6 Servings

6	pounds spareribs, cut into serving pieces
2	cups beer
¾	cup honey
1	teaspoon dry mustard
1	tablespoon chili powder
1	teaspoon crumbled sage
1	tablespoon salt
¼	cup lemon juice

Place the ribs into a roasting pan. In a bowl, combine the beer, honey, dry mustard, chili powder, sage, salt, and lemon juice. Pour this mixture over the ribs. Refrigerate the ribs for 12 or more hours, turning several times.

Remove the ribs from the marinade, reserving the liquid. Place the ribs on the grill, about 4 inches from the heat. Cook the ribs slowly, turning frequently and brushing with the marinade for about 1½ hours or until the ribs are brown and glazed.

"God made yeast, as well as dough, and loves fermentation just as dearly as he loves vegetation."

Ralph Waldo Emerson, American essayist, poet, and philosopher

CHAPTER 13

Steaks

❧ MARINATED GRILLED SIRLOIN ❧

· Yields 4 to 6 Servings

½	cup vegetable oil
12	ounces beer
¼	cup fresh lemon juice
½	cup ketchup
¼	teaspoon hot red pepper sauce
¼	cup honey
2	cloves garlic, finely chopped
2	teaspoons Dijon mustard
	Salt to taste
2½	pounds sirloin steak

In a casserole dish, beat the vegetable oil, beer, lemon juice, ketchup, pepper sauce, honey, garlic, mustard, and salt to taste together. Place the meat into the casserole and turn to coat it on all sides. Cover and marinate overnight, turning once.

Remove the meat from the dish, allowing the excess liquid to run off. Remove the marinade for basting.

Preheat the grill. Grill the steak for 8 to 10 minutes on each side, basting frequently. Let the meat rest for 10 minutes.

"PURE WATER IS THE BEST GIFTS A MAN CAN BRING. BUT WHO AM I THAT I SHOULD HAVE THE BEST OF ANYTHING? LET PRINCES REVEL AT THE PUMP, LET PEERS WITH PONDS MAKE FREE... BEER IS GOOD ENOUGH FOR ME."

Lord Neaves, Scottish writer

⁑⟨ BEER DIP & GRILLED STEAK ⟩⁑

· Yields 8 to 10 Servings

1	cup beer
¼	cup olive oil
1	clove garlic, minced
2	pounds sirloin steak (2-inch thick)
½	cup butter
1	teaspoon Worcestershire sauce
½	teaspoon dry mustard
2	tablespoons dry red wine
	Salt and pepper to taste

In a bowl, combine the beer, olive oil, and garlic. Place the steak into a casserole dish. Pour the beer mixture over the steak and refrigerate the steak in the marinade for 8 hours or overnight.

Preheat the grill. Remove the steak from the casserole, reserving the marinade. Grill the steak to the desired degree of doneness and cut it into bite-size pieces. Transfer the meat to a chafing dish and keep it warm.

In a saucepan, combine the butter, Worcestershire sauce, dry mustard, wine, and the remaining marinade. Cook the mixture over a medium heat until the butter is melted and the sauce is heated through. Adjust the seasonings, adding the salt and pepper to taste.

Serve the warm steak with the Beer Dip.

❋{ STEAK FAJITAS }❋

1½	pounds beef flank steak
12	ounces beer
2	tablespoons cooking oil
1	tablespoon coursely ground black pepper
2	teaspoons lime juice
2	cloves garlic, minced
½	teaspoon crushed dried oregano
12	flour or corn tortillas
1	large onion, chopped
2	tablespoons butter
1	16-ounce can refried beans, warmed
	Salsa
	Guacamole (optional)

Trim the excess fat from the steak and place the meat in a plastic bag in one bowl. In another bowl, combine the beer, cooking oil, pepper, lime juice, garlic, and oregano. Pour the mixture over the steak. Cover and refrigerate overnight, turning the bag occasionally.

Drain the steak, reserving the marinade. Pat the steak dry with the paper towels.

On a covered grill, cook the steak directly over medium-hot coals for 8 to 10 minutes, brushing the meat occasionally with the marinade. Turn and grill to the desired doneness. Carve the meat into thin slices.

Wrap the tortillas in the foil. Warm the tortillas in a 350° oven for 8 to 10 minutes.

In a skillet, cook the onions in the butter until they are tender.

Spread the tortillas with the refried beans and garnish with the onions, salsa, and guacamole. Wrap the steak slices in the tortillas.

❧ MARINATED & STUFFED FLANK STEAK ❧

· Yields 4 to 6 Servings

2	medium tomatoes, peeled and chopped
1	medium onion, chopped
2	garlic cloves, minced
1	teaspoon prepared mustard
1	teaspoon Worcestershire sauce
1/2	teaspoon dried thyme
1	tablespoon minced fresh parsley
	Salt and freshly ground pepper to taste
1	flank steak (about 2 pounds), trimmed of excess fat
1	cup beer
1	cup beef stock
	Melted butter
	Bread crumbs

Trim the flank steak of excess fat. In a medium bowl, combine the tomatoes, onion, garlic, mustard, Worcestershire sauce, and herbs. Add salt and pepper to taste. Spread this mixture on the side of the steak. Roll the steak carefully and tie it in 3 places. Place the steak in a large bowl and pour over equal amounts of beer and stock. Marinate the steak in the refrigerator for at least 8 hours, turning several times.

Place the steak roll and marinade into a pot and simmer for about 2 hours, until the meat is tender. Lift out the steak and brush it with butter, then with the bread crumbs. Bake the steak in a 375° oven for 15 minutes to brown the crumbs.

⋅⟩ BARBECUED FLANK STEAK ⟨⋅

· Yields 8 Servings

1	10.5-ounce can consommé
2/3	cup Soya sauce
1/2	cup chopped green onion
6	tablespoons lime juice
4	tablespoons brown sugar
1	clove garlic, crushed
2	large flank steaks
2	cups beer

In a medium bowl, combine the consommé, Soya sauce, onion, lime juice, brown sugar, and garlic, mixing well.

Place the flank steaks in a casserole dish and pour the mixture over them. Pour the beer over the flank steaks and marinate them for 24 hours.

Grill the flank steaks until desired doneness.

⋅⟩ MINUTE STEAKS ⟨⋅

· Yields 4 Servings

1	pound tenderized minute steaks (chipped steaks)
	Salt and freshly ground pepper to taste
1	tablespoon all-purpose flour
1/4	cup minced onion
1	cup beer
1/2	teaspoon granulated sugar
	Pinch of dried sage

In a skillet, season the steaks with the salt and pepper to taste. Brown the steaks over a high heat for 30 seconds on each side. Sprinkle the steaks with the flour on both sides. Add the onion, beer, sugar, and sage. Simmer, uncovered, until the beer evaporates into a thick sauce.

❧ GRILLED PEPPERED T-BONES ❧

· Yields 6 Servings

1	cup chopped onion
6	ounces beer
3/4	cup chili sauce
1/4	cup parsley
3	tablespoons Dijon mustard
1	tablespoon Worcestershire sauce
2	teaspoons brown sugar
1/2	teaspoon paprika
1/2	teaspoon freshly ground black pepper
3	beef T-bone steaks, cut 1-inch thick
1	to 1 1/2 teaspoons cracked black pepper

In a casserole dish, combine the onion, beer, chili sauce, parsley, mustard, Worcestershire sauce, brown sugar, paprika, and the 1/2 teaspoon of pepper. Place the steaks into the marinade. Cover and refrigerate for 4 to 6 hours or overnight, turning the steaks occasionally.

Remove the steaks from the marinade and then discard the marinade. Sprinkle both sides of the steaks with the cracked black pepper. Grill the steaks on an uncovered grill directly over medium-hot coals for 5 minutes. Turn and grill the steaks to the desired doneness, allowing 3 to 7 minutes for rare or 7 to 10 minutes for medium.

❧ BREADED VENISON STEAKS ❧

· Yields 4 to 6 Servings

6	eggs, beaten
1	to 2 tablespoons beer
	Seasoned salt to taste
	Pepper to taste
	Garlic salt to taste
1	to 2 pounds venison fillets
	Seasoned bread crumbs
4	tablespoons extra virgin olive oil
2	tablespoons butter

In one bowl, combine the eggs and beer. Add the seasoned salt, pepper, and garlic. Place the steaks in a baking dish and pour the marinade over the steaks. Cover the dish and allow it to marinate overnight or for at least 4 hours.

In another bowl, place the bread crumbs. Take the steaks out of the baking dish, place them in the bread crumbs, and coat them with the bread crumbs.

In a skillet, place the olive oil and butter and then heat. Once the skillet is warm, fry the steaks until desired doneness, which should be about 10 minutes.

"THE FIRST DRAUGHT SERVETH FOR HEALTH, THE SECOND FOR PLEASURE, THE THIRD FOR SHAME, THE FOURTH FOR MADNESS."

Sir Walter Raleigh, English poet and explorer

CHAPTER 14

Wild Game

❖⟨ BARBECUED VENISON ⟩❖

· Yields 6 Servings

12	ounces beer
3	cloves garlic
	Salt and pepper to taste
2	onions, sliced
3	bay leaves
3	pounds venison round steak (trim away excess fat)
2	cups barbecue sauce of choice

In a large bowl, combine the beer, garlic, salt, pepper, onions, and bay leaves, mixing well. Add the venison to the mixture, coating it completely. Refrigerate the venison for 12 hours to overnight, occasionally turning it.

Remove the venison and onions from the marinade and place them in a crock-pot. Pour 1 cup of the barbecue sauce over the venison and cover the crock-pot. Cook the venison on low for 11 hours or until desired doneness.

Serve the venison with the remaining barbecue sauce.

"They who drink beer will think beer."

Washington Irving, American author

❊{ VENISON SWISS STEAK }❊

· Yields 4 to 6 Servings

½	cup all-purpose flour (for dredging)
½	teaspoon salt (for dredging)
½	teaspoon pepper (for dredging)
3	pounds venison round steak, ¾- to 1-inch thick, cut 3 x 4-inches
	Mustard powder to taste
½	cup bacon grease
1	10¾-ounce can stewed tomatoes
1	medium onion, finely chopped
1	large carrot, finely chopped
12	ounces beer
1	tablespoon Worcestershire sauce
½	teaspoon ground thyme
2	cups beef bouillon
1	tablespoon brown sugar
	Salt and pepper to taste

In a medium bowl, combine the flour, the ½ teaspoon of salt, and the ½ teaspoon of pepper, mixing well. Dredge the venison steaks in the flour mixture. Sprinkle the mustard powder over the venison steaks.

In a skillet, brown the venison steaks in the bacon grease.

In a medium bowl, combine the tomatoes, onion, carrot, beer, Worcestershire sauce, thyme, bouillon, brown sugar, salt, and pepper, mixing well.

Place the venison steaks in a casserole dish and cover them with the beer mixture. Add water or other liquid stock, making sure that the venison steaks are covered. Bake the venison steaks, covered, at 300° for 2½ to 3 hours until the venison steaks are tender.

Remove the lid and continue baking until the sauce is thick.

❧ STUFFED ELK STEAKS ❧

· Yields 4 Servings

For the Steaks:

4	½-pound steaks (butterflied loin or round steak) (Elk, venison, or beef)
½	bottle beer
2	cups (1 pound) butter
2	teaspoons chicken or beef bouillon
1	large onion, diced
2	cups chopped celery or fresh celery leaves
	Salt and pepper to taste

Place the steaks in a roaster. Pour the beer over and around the steaks. Add the butter. Sprinkle the bouillon in the beer and on the steaks. Place the onions and celery around the steaks. Cover the steaks with aluminum foil and place the lid on the roaster (the aluminum foil will create steam around the steaks, allowing them to simmer; without the aluminum foil and only the lid, the steaks will burn). Place the roaster on burners on top of the stove over a medium heat, frying them until the steaks begin turning brown. Remove the steaks from the roaster and pat them dry with paper towels.

For the Stuffing:

15	slices white bread, cubed and without the crusts
½	medium onion + 3 ribs celery, combined in a blender and finely chopped
	Seasoned salt to taste
	Seasoned pepper to taste
1	teaspoon beef bouillon (or to taste)
1	egg

To make the stuffing, combine all of the stuffing ingredients, mixing well.

Using the same roaster, leave all of the juices on the bottom. Stuff the steaks with the stuffing, season them on both sides with the salt and pepper to taste, and wrap them individually in aluminum foil. Place a rack in the roaster and place the steaks on top of the rack, keeping them away from the juices on the bottom. Bake the steaks at 350° for approximately 1½ hours.

If the juices on the bottom of the roaster begin to dry up, add water. Turn the steaks over and bake them for another hour or until desired doneness.

For the Gravy:

Strain the juice from the roaster after the steaks are finished and transfer to a saucepan. Add more water or beer if necessary. Bring to a boil.

Combine 1 cup of flour with enough water to create a liquid paste with no lumps. Boil the reserved juice and slowly add the flour mixture, mixing well. Continue stirring the gravy until it thickens to the desired consistency and is heated through. Serve the gravy on top of or alongside the Stuffed Elk Steaks.

"WHO'D CARE TO BE A BEE AND SIP
SWEET HONEY FROM THE FLOWER'S LIP
WHEN HE MIGHT BE A FLY AND STEER
HEAD FIRST INTO A CAN OF BEER?"

Anonymous

❧ BARBECUED ELK ROAST ❧

· Yields 4 to 6 Servings

12	ounces beer
3	cloves garlic
	Salt and pepper to taste
2	onions, sliced
3	bay leaves
3	pounds elk round, leg, or rump roast (trim away excess fat)
2	cups barbecue sauce

In a large bowl, combine the beer, garlic, salt, pepper, onions, and bay leaves, mixing well. Add the elk roast, covering it with the marinade. Refrigerate the elk roast for 12 to 24 hours, turning it occasionally.

Remove the elk roast and onions from the marinade. Place the elk roast and onions in a crock-pot. Pour 1 cup of the barbecue sauce over the elk roast. Cook the elk roast on low for 10 to 12 hours.

Serve the Barbecued Elk Roast with the remaining barbecue sauce.

❧ TANGY BARBECUE ELK BRISKET ❧

· Yields 4 to 6 Servings

2	to 3 pounds elk brisket
	Salt and pepper to taste
¼	cup oil
¾	cup beer
½	cup packed brown sugar

For the Barbecue Sauce:

2	tablespoons butter
2	cloves garlic, minced
1	large onion, chopped
½	cup Worcestershire sauce
¼	cup apple cider vinegar
¼	cup beer
1¾	cups ketchup
	Tabasco sauce to taste
	Dash of cayenne pepper
½	teaspoon dry mustard
¼	teaspoon salt
2	tablespoons brown sugar
	Pinch of celery seed
	Pinch of ground cloves
	Pinch of grated nutmeg
	Pinch of paprika

In a medium skillet, combine the butter, garlic, and onion, sautéing the garlic and onion until they are limp. Add all of the remaining barbecue sauce ingredients and bring them to a boil. Turn the heat down and simmer the mixture, uncovered, for 15 minutes.

Preheat the oven to 350°. Season the brisket with the salt and pepper to taste. In another skillet, combine the oil and brisket, browning the brisket on both sides. Place the brisket in a large roasting pan and cover it liberally with the barbecue sauce. Add the beer and sprinkle the brown sugar on top. Bake the elk brisket, covered, for 2½ hours or until tender, basting it frequently.

Serve the elk brisket with the sauce over mashed potatoes.

❧ LAMB ❧

· Yields 6 Servings

2	teaspoons grated ginger
1	teaspoon cayenne pepper
1	tablespoon rosemary
2	tablespoons Dijon mustard
1	teaspoon garlic powder
1/4	teaspoon paprika
	Salt and pepper to taste
1/2	cup beer
5	pounds leg of lamb, butterflied

In a blender, combine the ginger, cayenne pepper, rosemary, mustard, garlic powder, paprika, salt, pepper, and 1 tablespoon of the beer, mixing well until the mixture forms a paste. Rub half of the mixture on the inside of the lamb. Roll and tie the lamb, rubbing the remainder of the paste on the outside of the lamb. Place the lamb in a roasting pan and pour the remainder of the beer over it. Bake the lamb, covered, at 350° for approximately 2 hours or until desired doneness.

❧ BEAR STEAKS ❧

· Yields 4 Servings

2 1/4	cups beer
1	large onion, sliced
6	tablespoons oil
2	tablespoons Worcestershire sauce
2	cloves garlic, minced
3	pounds bone-in bear steak

½	cup beef broth
1	8-ounce can tomatoes, cut-up
½	cup chopped carrots
½	cup chopped celery
½	teaspoon crushed dried basil
½	teaspoon prepared mustard
½	teaspoon salt
⅛	teaspoon pepper
2	tablespoons cornstarch
2	tablespoons water
	Hot cooked noodles

In a medium bowl, combine 1½ cups of the beer, onion, 4 tablespoons of the oil, Worcestershire sauce, and garlic, mixing well. Pierce the bear steak with a fork. Place the bear steak in a plastic bag within a shallow pan. Pour the marinade over the bag and then seal the bag. Chill the bear steak for several hours, turning it occasionally. Drain the bag, discarding the marinade.

In a skillet, combine the meat and remaining 2 tablespoons of hot oil, browning the bear steak on both sides. Add ¾ cup of the beer, beef broth, tomatoes, carrots, celery, basil, mustard, salt, and pepper to the meat, bringing the mixture to a boil. Reduce the heat and simmer the mixture, covered, for 1½ hours or until the meat is tender. Transfer the meat to a platter.

Skim the fat off of the pan juices. In a blender, combine the cornstarch and water, mixing well. Stir this mixture into the pan juices. Cook and stir the mixture until it is thickened. Cook the mixture for 1 to 2 more minutes. Serve the bear steak and sauce with noodles.

"BEER DRINKING DOESN'T DO HALF THE HARM OF LOVEMAKING."

Eden Philpotts, English author

❖⟩ GRILLED RABBIT ⟨❖

· Yields 6 Servings

3	pounds rabbit meat
2	tablespoons garlic salt
12	ounces beer

Place the rabbit on a heated grill and season it with the garlic salt. Cook the rabbit for 15 minutes. Baste the rabbit with the beer every 10 minutes for approximately 30 minutes or until desired doneness.

❖⟩ RABBIT ⟨❖

· Yields 4 Servings

1	3-pound domestic rabbit, cut-up
	Salt and pepper to taste
2	tablespoons oil
4	medium potatoes, quartered
4	medium carrots, cut into ½-inch pieces
1	medium onion, sliced
12	ounces beer
¼	cup chili sauce
½	teaspoon salt
¼	cup cold water
2	tablespoons all-purpose flour

Season the rabbit with the salt and pepper to taste. In a skillet, combine the oil and rabbit, browning the rabbit on all sides. Drain the fat. Add the potatoes, carrots, and onion.

In a medium bowl, combine the beer, chili sauce, and the ½ teaspoon of salt, mixing well. Pour the mixture over the rabbit and vegetables in the skillet. Bring the mixture to a boil and then reduce the heat. Simmer the mixture, covered, for 35 to 45 minutes or until the meat is tender. Remove the rabbit and vegetables. Keep them warm.

For the sauce, skim the fat from the pan juices. If necessary, add water to the juices to equal 1½ cups. Return the pan juices to the skillet. In a small bowl, combine the ¼ cup of water and flour, mixing well. Stir the flour mixture into the pan juices. Cook and stir the mixture until it is thickened and bubbly. Cook and stir the mixture for 1 more minute. Serve the sauce with the rabbit and vegetables.

·{ SQUIRREL DINNER FOR TWO }·

· Yields 2 Servings

2	squirrels, cleaned well
2	tablespoons salt
2	large sweet onions, sliced
4	carrots, halved
	Salt and pepper to taste
2	cloves fresh garlic, chopped (or 1 teaspoon garlic powder), sprinkled over the squirrel
1	10¾-ounce can cream of mushroom soup
1	cup water
¼	cup beer

Place the squirrels in a large bowl. Add enough water, plus the 2 tablespoons of salt, to cover the squirrels. Cover and let set in refrigerator overnight.

Drain off the water and rinse the squirrels. Pat the meat dry. Place the onions in the bottom of a roasting pan. Add the squirrels, carrots, and seasonings.

In a bowl, combine the cream of mushroom soup, 1 cup of water, and beer, mixing well. Pour the soup mixture over the squirrels. Roast the squirrels, covered, at 325° for 2½ hours or until the meat is tender.

❧ GRILLED DOVE ❧

· Yields 1 Serving

½	cup Italian dressing
½	cup red wine
6	dove breasts (use 10 to 12 dove breasts for 2 servings)
¼	cup beer
	Salt and pepper to taste
	Seasoned salt to taste
	Red pepper to taste
1	tablespoon olive oil (if using frying pan)
1	tablespoon butter (if using frying pan)

In a large bowl, pour the Italian dressing and red wine over the dove breasts. Add the beer. Season the dove breasts with the salt, pepper, seasoned salt, and red pepper to taste. Cover the bowl and refrigerate, marinating the mixture for 4 to 5 hours. Remove the dove breasts and reserve the marinade.

Over a medium heat, grill the dove breasts until they are golden. Or, coat a frying pan with the olive oil and butter. Then, in the frying pan, cook the dove breasts for about 8 to 10 minutes, turning them often or until the center is light pink.

In a large saucepan, bring the marinade to a boil. Add the grilled dove breasts, reduce the heat, and simmer the mixture for 15 minutes or until desired doneness.

"PAYDAY came and with it beer."

Rudyard Kipling, English author and poet

❖{ DRUNK DUCK }❖

· Yields 4 to 6 Servings

5	pounds duck meat, cut into serving pieces
1	tablespoon safflower oil
1	large onion, thickly sliced
2	1-inch long pieces lemon peel
3	cloves garlic, minced
1	teaspoon crushed cumin seeds
	Salt and pepper to taste
1½	cups chopped cilantro
3	cups chicken stock
3	cups beer
2	cups raw long-grained rice

Prick the duck skin all over with a fork. In a skillet, combine the safflower oil, duck, and onion, sautéing the duck and onion over a medium-high heat until the duck meat is browned on all sides and the onion is golden. Drain off the fat.

Add the lemon peel, garlic, cumin, salt, pepper, ¾ cup of the cilantro, chicken stock, and beer, mixing well. Bring the mixture to a boil. Lower the heat and simmer the mixture, covered, for approximately 45 minutes until the duck is very tender.

Remove the duck to a hot platter and keep it warm. Drain off the liquid and measure 3½ cups. Add the rice to the skillet with the measured cooking liquid. Cook the rice, covered, for about 20 minutes until the rice is tender and has absorbed all of the liquid. Serve the duck and rice together on a platter. Garnish with the rest of the cilantro.

❊⟨ STEWED DUCK ⟩❊

· Yields 4 Servings

5	pounds duck meat, cut into serving pieces
	Salt
	Marjoram
	All-purpose flour
3	to 4 tablespoons butter
½	cup beer
¾	to 1 cup hot chicken stock
1	clove garlic
¼	onion
1	bay leaf
1	small piece lemon rind
1	rib celery
3	sprigs parsley
¼	teaspoon thyme
2	tablespoons all-purpose flour + 3 tablespoons water
¼	teaspoon anchovy paste

Sprinkle the duck lightly with the salt and a little marjoram and dredge it in the flour.

In a covered skillet, heat the butter until it is bubbling. Add the duck, browning it on all sides. Pour in the beer, let it sizzle up for a minute or so, and then add the chicken stock. Add the garlic, onion, bay leaf, lemon rind, celery, parsley, and thyme, stirring to combine. Simmer the mixture, covered, for about 40 minutes or until the duck is tender.

Remove the vegetables, bay leaf, and lemon rind. Skim the fat from the juice. Stir in the flour and water mixture. Stir in the anchovy paste and season the mixture to taste.

Place the duck on a heated platter and pour the gravy over it.

❧ GOOSE ☙

· Yields 4 to 6 Servings

4	medium potatoes, scrubbed and halved
3	or 4 carrots, bias-cut into 1-inch pieces
1	onion, thinly sliced
½	goose, skinned, filleted, and cut into 2-inch cubes
1	cup beer
¼	cup barbecue sauce
2	tablespoons brown sugar
½	teaspoon garlic salt

In a crock-pot, combine the potatoes, carrots, and onion. Place the goose on top.

In a small bowl, combine the beer, barbecue sauce, brown sugar, and garlic salt, mixing well. Pour this mixture over the goose. Cook the goose, covered, on medium for 6 to 8 hours.

"Cold beer, hot lights
My sweet romantic teenage nights."
Billy Joel, American singer, "Scenes from an Italian Restaurant"

❧ FRIED PHEASANT STRIPS ❧

· Yields 2 to 4 Servings

1	cup all-purpose flour
1	cup cornmeal
12	ounces beer (or less)
1	pheasant breast, boned and cut into 2-inch strips
	Salt and pepper to taste

In a medium bowl, combine the flour and cornmeal, mixing well. Add the beer, creating a thick batter. Place the pheasant strips in the batter, coating them completely.

In a skillet, fry the pheasant strips until they are golden.

"MOST PEOPLE HATE THE TASTE OF BEER—
TO BEGIN WITH. IT IS, HOWEVER, A PREJU-
DICE THAT MANY PEOPLE HAVE BEEN ABLE
TO OVERCOME."

Winston Churchill, British Prime Minister

CHAPTER 15

Stews

❧ MICROWAVABLE BEEF STEW ❧

· Yields 6 Servings

4	slices bacon, cut into ½-inch pieces
1½	pounds boneless round steak, cut into 1-inch pieces
4	medium onions, sliced
1	clove garlic, minced
12	ounces beer
⅓	cup all-purpose flour
1	tablespoon packed brown sugar
1½	teaspoons salt
½	teaspoon dried thyme leaves
¼	teaspoon pepper
1	tablespoon vinegar
	Snipped parsley
3½	to 4½ cups hot cooked noodles

Place the bacon into a casserole dish. Cover with paper towels. Microwave the bacon on high for 2 minutes. Cover and microwave the bacon for 3 or 4 minutes longer until it is crisp.

Drain the bacon on paper towels. Pour off the fat, returning 2 tablespoons of the fat to the casserole. Stir in the beef, onions, and garlic. Cover the casserole tightly and microwave on high for 6 minutes. Stir. Cover and microwave the dish 5 to 7 minutes longer until the beef is no longer pink.

Stir in the beer, flour, brown sugar, salt, thyme, and pepper. Cover tightly and microwave on medium-low for 30 minutes. Stir. Cover and microwave the beef for 25 to 30 minutes longer until the beef is tender.

Stir in the vinegar and sprinkle the stew with bacon and parsley. Serve with the noodles.

❈ SAUSAGE STEW ❈

· Yields 8 Servings

1	pound smoked sausage, cut into 1-inch pieces
8	small new potatoes, halved
16	ounces baby carrots
12	ounces beer
½	cup water
2	cubes beef bouillon
⅛	teaspoon thyme
⅛	teaspoon basil
½	teaspoon minced garlic
1	teaspoon minced onion

In a saucepan, combine all of the ingredients. Heat the mixture to boiling over a medium-high heat, stirring occasionally. Reduce the mixture to a low heat, cover, and simmer for 20 minutes.

"And the air was such a wonder
From the hot-dogs and the beer.
Yes, there used to be a ballpark right here."

Frank Sinatra, American singer, "There Used To Be A Ballpark"

❧ LIGHT BEER BEEF STEW ❧

· Yields 4 Servings

1	pound lean round steak
	Vegetable cooking spray
1	teaspoon vegetable oil
1	cup chopped onion
12	ounces light beer
2	bay leaves
½	teaspoon dried whole thyme
½	teaspoon freshly ground pepper
¼	teaspoon salt
5	medium carrots, cut into ½-inch slices
½	pound fresh mushrooms
2	teaspoons cornstarch
2	tablespoons water

Trim the excess fat from the steak. Slice the steak across the grain into thin strips.

Coat a Dutch oven with the cooking spray. Add the oil and place the Dutch oven over a medium-high heat until hot. Add the meat to the Dutch oven. Cook the meat until it is browned. Reduce the heat to medium-low. Add the onion and cook for 10 minutes or until the onion is tender and lightly browned. Stir in the light beer, bay leaves, thyme, pepper, salt, carrots, and mushrooms. Bring the mixture to a boil. Cover, reduce the heat, and simmer for 1 to 1½ hours or until the meat is tender.

In a bowl, combine the cornstarch and water, stirring until blended. Stir this mixture into the meat mixture. Cook, uncovered, for 10 more minutes, stirring occasionally. Remove and discard the bay leaves.

⁂{ VEGETABLE STEW }⁂

• Yields 12 Servings

3	cups water, lightly salted
½	rib celery
10	carrots, peeled and cut-up
1	medium white onion, halved
2	large potatoes, cut into bite-size pieces
1	large turnip, peeled and cut-up
1	green bell pepper
1	red bell pepper (optional)
2	jalapeño peppers, halved lengthwise
3	cloves garlic (2 smashed and 1 whole)
1	15-ounce can whole kernel corn
1	15-ounce can English peas
1	15-ounce can baby lima beans
1	14.5-ounce can chicken broth
	Beer (warm and as needed)
	Pepper to taste
	Dill weed to taste
1	large purple onion, chopped

In a large pot, combine the salted water and celery. Bring the water to a boil for 2 minutes. Simmer the mixture, uncovered, while adding the carrots, white onion, potatoes, turnip, green and red bell peppers, jalapeño peppers, garlic, corn, peas, lima beans, and chicken broth, mixing well.

Add the beer as needed for more liquid. Add the pepper to taste. Add the dill weed to taste. Cook the mixture on high, continually stirring. Add the purple onion. Bring the mixture to a boil and then cook it, covered, over a low heat.

Once the Vegetable Stew is thoroughly heated, serve it with whole wheat bread or another favorite side dish.

❧ ST. PATRICK'S DAY STEW ❧

· Yields 6 to 8 Servings

1	tablespoon olive oil
1	onion, chopped
1½	pounds lean boneless lamb shoulders, cut into ¾-inch cubes
12	ounces beer
1	teaspoon pepper
2	14-ounce cans broth
1	.87-ounce envelope brown gravy mix
3	cups cubed potatoes
2	cups thinly sliced carrots
	Chopped parsley (to garnish)

In a skillet, combine the olive oil and onion, sautéing the onion until it is brown. Add the lamb and continue to sauté the mixture until the meat is browned. Stir in the beer and pepper. Simmer the meat, covered, for 30 minutes.

Add the broth and gravy mix, mixing well. Add the potatoes and carrots. Simmer the meat, covered, for approximately 15 minutes until the vegetables are tender. Garnish each serving with the parsley.

"WORK IS THE CURSE OF THE DRINKING CLASS."

Oscar Wilde, Irish playwright and author

❖{ PORK STEW }❖

· Yields 6 to 8 Servings

1	tablespoon olive oil
2	pounds boneless pork shoulder, trimmed of fat and cut into 1-inch cubes
1	medium onion, chopped
2	cloves garlic, chopped
1	8¼-ounce can whole tomatoes
1	red serrano chile pepper, finely chopped
2	tablespoons snipped fresh cilantro
1	teaspoon salt
1	teaspoon ground cumin
½	teaspoon dried oregano leaves
12	ounces beer
1	red pepper, cut into small pieces

In a Dutch oven, heat the olive oil until it is hot. Add the pork and cook it, covered, for approximately 25 minutes over a medium heat, stirring frequently, until the liquid has evaporated and the pork is browned.

Remove the pork with a slotted spoon. Drain all but 2 tablespoons of the fat from the Dutch oven. In the Dutch oven, sauté the onion and garlic until the onion is tender. Add the tomatoes, chile pepper, cilantro, salt, cumin, and oregano, stirring well. Break-up the tomatoes with a fork and bring the mixture to a boil. Reduce the heat and simmer the mixture, uncovered, for 10 minutes.

Stir in the pork, beer, and red pepper. Bring the mixture to a boil, reduce the heat, and simmer it, uncovered, for about 15 minutes until the pork is tender and the sauce is thickened.

❈⦃ LAMB STEW ⦄❈

· Yields 8 Servings

16	ounces navy beans, drained
16	ounces garbanzo beans, drained
1	pound boneless lamb, cut into ¾-inch cubes
12	ounces beer
1	cup chicken broth
½	cup chopped onion
1	clove garlic, minced
½	teaspoon salt
⅛	teaspoon pepper
3	cups peeled and cubed potatoes or turnips
8	ounces whole kernel corn, drained
2	tablespoons snipped parsley

In a Dutch oven, combine the navy and garbanzo beans, lamb, beer, broth, onion, garlic, salt, and pepper, mixing well. Bring the mixture to a boil. Simmer the mixture, covered, for 45 minutes or until the meat is nearly tender.

Add the potatoes or turnips and corn. Simmer the mixture, covered, for 15 minutes or until the meat and vegetables are done. Stir in the parsley. Season to taste.

"I drink, therefore I am."

Anonymous

❊⟨ BEEF STEW ⟩❊

· Yields 2 Servings

4	pounds lean beef, cut into 1 x 2-inch slices
½	cup all-purpose flour
½	cup vegetable oil
2	pounds large onions, thickly sliced
6	cloves garlic, crushed
3	tablespoons firmly packed brown sugar
¼	cup red wine vinegar, divided
½	cup chopped fresh parsley
2	small bay leaves
2	teaspoons dried thyme
1	tablespoon salt
	Freshly ground black pepper
2	10½-ounce cans condensed beef broth
3	cups beer

Preheat the oven to 325°. Coat the beef strips with the flour. In a skillet, heat the oil and brown the strips a few at a time. Place the strips in a large casserole dish and set it aside.

In the skillet, brown the onions and garlic. Add the onions and garlic to the casserole. Add the brown sugar, 2 tablespoons of the red wine vinegar, parsley, bay leaves, thyme, salt, and pepper, stirring to combine the ingredients.

Pour off any oil remaining in the skillet. Add the broth and heat it over a low heat, stirring to loosen all browned bits. Pour the mixture over the strips and add the beer. Bake the strips, covered, at 350° for 2 hours.

Take the casserole out of the oven and place it on top of the stove. Stir in the remaining 2 tablespoons of red wine vinegar. Remove the bay leaf and cook the strips over a medium heat until the sauce bubbles. Serve with dumplings or rice.

✳❦ ELK STEW ❦✳

· Yields 6 to 8 Servings

1½	pounds elk meat (cut-up roast or stew meat)
1	10¾-ounce can cream of mushroom soup
1	1-ounce package dry onion soup mix
8	ounces beer
1	cup diced fresh or canned tomatoes
6	to 8 small onions, chopped
4	to 6 potatoes, cut into bite-size pieces
2	to 3 ribs celery, cut into bite-size pieces
2	to 3 carrots, cut into bite-size pieces
1	teaspoon Worcestershire sauce

In a crock-pot, combine all of the ingredients, mixing well. Cook the stew on low for 8 hours or until the desired doneness.

"I'VE GOT FRIENDS IN LOW PLACES
WHERE THE WHISKEY DROWNS AND THE
BEER CHASES
MY BLUES AWAY."

Garth Brooks, American country music singer, "Low Places"

CHAPTER 16

Freshwater Fish

❋{ HADDOCK }❋

· Yields 4 to 6 Servings

	Oil for deep frying
1	cup all-purpose flour
¼	teaspoon paprika
½	teaspoon salt
⅛	teaspoon pepper
¾	cup beer
2	pounds haddock, cleaned and rinsed

Preheat the oil in a deep fryer to 375°. In a bowl, combine the flour, paprika, salt, and pepper. Gradually stir in the beer with a whisk, beating until the mixture is smooth.

Dip the haddock into the beer batter, coating the fillets completely. Lower the haddock into the hot oil, frying only a few at a time, for 2 to 3 minutes or until they are golden brown. Drain the haddock on paper towels and serve.

"Big Kosher pickle and a cold draft beer
Well good God Almighty which way do I steer . . ."

Jimmy Buffet, American singer, "Cheeseburger in Paradise"

❧ CRAPPIE ❧

· Yields 8 Servings

	Oil for deep frying
1½	cups Bisquick mix
1	egg, beaten
1½	cups beer
1	teaspoon salt
8	crappie fillets

Preheat the oil in a deep fryer to 375°. In a bowl, combine the Bisquick mix, egg, beer, and salt. Mix until smooth. Dip the crappie into the beer batter, coating the fillets completely. Lower the crappie into the hot oil, frying only a few at a time, for 2 to 3 minutes or until they are golden brown. Drain the crappie on paper towels and serve.

❧ WALLEYE ❧

· Yields 2 Servings

¼	cup cornstarch
¼	cup all-purpose flour
¼	cup beer
2	egg whites
2	walleye fillets
	Oil for deep frying

In a medium bowl, sift together the cornstarch and flour. Add the beer, mixing well until the mixture is smooth. In a medium bowl, beat the egg whites until stiff. Fold the beer batter into the egg whites. Completely coat the walleye fillets. Deep-fry or pan-fry the walleye fillets until they are well-browned on both sides.

❧ TROUT ❧

· Yields 6 Servings

1	cup all-purpose flour
1	cup cornstarch
1	teaspoon baking powder
1	teaspoon cayenne pepper
12	ounces beer
2	pounds trout fillets
	Oil for frying

In a bowl, combine the flour, cornstarch, baking powder, and cayenne pepper. Add the beer, mixing well. Dip the trout into the beer batter, coating the fillets completely. In the skillet, fry the trout in the oil until they are a golden brown. Drain the trout on paper towels and serve.

"ALE IT IS CALLED AMONG MEN, AND AMONG GODS, BEER."

First recorded mention of the word "ale" occurred around 950 A.D. in the Old Norse "Alvismal"

❖{ SWEET & SOUR TROUT }❖

· Yields 10 Servings

¼	cup butter
2	onions, chopped
2	tablespoons all-purpose flour
12	ounces beer
2	tablespoons packed brown sugar
5	peppercorns
2	whole cloves
1	teaspoon Worcestershire sauce
3	pounds trout fillets, cut into bite-size pieces
1	tablespoon vinegar

In a skillet, combine the butter and onions, sautéing the onions until they are tender. Add the flour and cook the mixture, uncovered, for 3 minutes. Add the beer, brown sugar, peppercorns, cloves, and Worcestershire sauce, cooking over a low heat and stirring until the mixture is thickened. Add the trout fillets and cook the mixture, covered, until the fillets are done. Add the vinegar and cook for 2 minutes longer.

"Roll out those lazy, hazy, crazy days of summer
Those days of soda and pretzels and beer."
Nat King Cole, American singer, "Those Lazy, Hazy, Crazy Days of Summer"

❖❴ CLAY POT SALMON ❵❖

· Yields 4 Servings

4	salmon steaks
2	tablespoons butter, melted
¼	cup parsley
½	teaspoon salt
1	clove garlic, crushed
1	teaspoon lemon juice
½	cup beer
1	teaspoon arrowroot

Presoak a clay pot, top and bottom, in water for 15 minutes.

Place the salmon steaks into the pot.

In a bowl, combine the butter, parsley, salt, garlic, lemon juice, and beer. Pour the mixture over the salmon. Cover the pot and place it in a cold oven. Set the oven temperature at 450°. Cook the salmon for 30 minutes.

Remove the pot from the oven and pour off the liquid into the saucepan. Return the pot to the oven, without a lid, for 5 more minutes until the salmon is browned. Heat the liquid and thicken it slightly with the arrowroot. Pour the liquid over the salmon and serve.

❄❴ WHITE PERCH ❵❄

· Yields 4 Servings

4	tablespoons all-purpose flour
2	tablespoons yellow cornmeal
½	teaspoon dill weed
1	teaspoon salt
1	tablespoon paprika
3	ounces beer
4	white perch fillets, scaled and sprinkled inside and outside with lemon juice
4	tablespoons oil

In a medium bowl, combine the flour, cornmeal, dill weed, salt, and paprika, mixing well. Add the beer, mixing until the mixture is smooth. Coat the white perch with the beer batter. In a skillet, sauté the white perch in the oil for approximately 8 minutes on each side or until desired doneness.

"THE BEST PLACE TO DRINK BEER IS AT HOME. OR ON A RIVER BANK, IF THE FISH DON'T BOTHER YOU."

American folk saying

⁘{ CATFISH }⁘

· Yields 1 Serving

3	tablespoons butter
5	cloves garlic, chopped
5	green onions, chopped
2	catfish fillets, lightly floured
4	mushrooms, sliced
3	ounces beer
	Juice from ½ lemon
	Worcestershire sauce (or to taste)
	Cooked white rice

In a skillet, combine the butter, garlic, and onions, sautéing the garlic and onions until they are browned. Add the catfish and mushrooms. Pour in the beer and lemon juice. Add a couple drops of the Worcestershire sauce. Sauté the catfish over a medium heat, turning the fillets, until they are browned on both sides. Serve the catfish with the white rice.

"BEER: BECAUSE ONE DOESN'T SOLVE THE WORLD'S PROBLEMS OVER WHITE WINE."

Anonymous

❖{ COD }❖

· Yields 4 Servings

1	egg
1½	cups beer
1	cup all-purpose flour
1	teaspoon garlic powder
½	teaspoon salt
½	teaspoon ground black pepper
1	pound cod fillets
2	cups crushed cornflake crumbs
1	teaspoon Cajun seasoning
	Oil for frying

In a medium bowl, combine the egg, beer, flour, garlic powder, salt, and pepper, beating until the mixture is smooth. Completely coat the cod fillets with the batter. In another medium bowl, combine the cornflake crumbs and Cajun seasoning, mixing well. Completely coat the cod fillets with the crumb mixture. In a skillet or deep fryer, heat the oil to 365° and fry the cod fillets until they are golden.

"There are those who drink and those who pound,
and those who don't are bound to frown.
No matter what you say or what you do,
Always cheer your frosty brew!"

Anonymous

❧ BASS ❧

· Yields 6 Servings

4	tablespoons vegetable oil
1	large onion, diced
2	tablespoons all-purpose flour
1½	cups beer
2	tablespoons brown sugar
¼	teaspoon pepper
2	teaspoons Worcestershire sauce
3	pounds bass, cut into 6 fillets

In a skillet, combine the oil and onion, sautéing the onion until it is translucent. Add the flour, mixing well. Cook the mixture, covered, for 2 minutes. Add the beer, brown sugar, pepper, and Worcestershire sauce, mixing well. Heat the mixture until it thickens.

Place the bass fillets in the skillet and cook them until they easily flake.

❧ FLOUNDER ❧

· Yields 4 Servings

2	pounds flounder fillets
	Olive oil
3	cups grated bread crumbs
2	cups diced American cheese
2	teaspoons paprika
2	teaspoons mustard powder
4	teaspoons Worcestershire sauce
1	cup beer

Brush the flounder fillets with the olive oil. Roll the flounder fillets in the bread crumbs. Broil the flounder fillets for approximately 4 minutes on both sides.

In a saucepan, combine the American cheese, paprika, mustard powder, Worcestershire sauce, and beer, mixing well. Cook the mixture over a low heat, stirring until the cheese melts and then whip the mixture until it is smooth.

Place the flounder fillets on a platter and pour the beer sauce over them.

❧ BEER-POACHED FISH ❧

· Yields 4 Servings

1	tablespoon chopped parsley
1	teaspoon salt
1/4	teaspoon pepper
1	teaspoon chopped dill weed
1	onion, chopped
4	lemon slices
1	cup beer
1 1/2	pounds fish fillets

In a skillet, combine 1-inch of water with all of the ingredients, except the fish fillets, mixing well. Bring the mixture to a boil. Add the fish fillets, arranging them in a single layer in the skillet. Simmer the mixture, covered, for approximately 5 minutes or until the fish fillets flake easily.

❧ MARINATED FISH STEAKS ❧

· Yields 4 Servings

12	ounces beer
½	cup oil
1	clove garlic, chopped
2	tablespoons lime juice
1	tablespoon brown sugar
1	teaspoon salt
3	whole cloves
4	fish steaks

In a medium bowl, combine all of the ingredients, except the fish steaks, mixing well. Pour this mixture into a shallow pan. Add the fish steaks to the marinade and let the mixture stand for at least 1 hour, turning the fish steaks several times.

Drain the steaks. Either grill or pan-fry the fish steaks, browning them on both sides, until desired doneness.

"WITHOUT QUESTION, THE GREATEST INVENTION IN THE HISTORY OF MANKIND IS BEER. OH, I GRANT YOU THAT THE WHEEL WAS A FINE INVENTION, BUT THE WHEEL DOES NOT GO NEARLY AS WELL WITH PIZZA."

Dave Barry, American humorist and author

❊⟩ FISH FRY ⟨❊

· Yields 4 to 6 Servings

2	pounds white-fleshed fish fillets, halved or quartered
	Vinegar or lemon juice
	Salt to taste
⅔	cup all-purpose flour
1	egg, lightly beaten
½	cup beer
	Oil for deep frying

In one bowl, sprinkle the fillets with vinegar or lemon juice. Marinate for 30 minutes.

With paper towels, pat the fillets dry and sprinkle with salt to taste.

In another bowl, combine the flour, egg, and salt to taste. Add the beer. With a fork, stir the beer batter until it is blended and free of lumps, but not too thin.

Preheat the oil in a deep fryer to 375°. Set the wire basket into the hot oil. Dip the fillets into the beer batter, coating them completely. Slip the fillets into the hot oil, frying only a few at a time. Fry the fillets for 6 to 8 minutes or until they are golden brown. Drain the fillets on paper towels and serve.

"24 HOURS IN A DAY. 24 BEERS IN A CASE. COINCIDENCE? I THINK NOT."

Steven Wright, American comedian

❊{ FISH NUGGETS }❊

· Yields 4 Servings

3	eggs, slightly beaten
½	cup milk
½	cup beer
3	tablespoons mustard
½	teaspoon Tabasco sauce
2	tablespoons salt, divided
2	teaspoons pepper, divided
2	pounds fish fillets, cut into bite-size pieces
3	cups fine yellow corn flour
	Vegetable oil

In a medium bowl, combine the eggs, milk, beer, mustard, Tabasco sauce, half of the salt, and half of the pepper, whisking the mixture well. Completely coat the fish nuggets with the batter, place them in a bowl, cover, and refrigerate them for 1 hour.

In another medium bowl, combine the corn flour and the remaining salt and pepper, mixing well.

Preheat the vegetable oil in a deep fryer to 370°. Dredge the fish nuggets in the corn flour mixture. Fry the fish nuggets until they float on the surface and turn golden, being careful not to overcook them. Drain the fish nuggets on paper towels and pat them to absorb the excess oil.

CHAPTER 17

❊⟩ BEER-BATTERED SHRIMP ⟨❊

· Yields 6 Servings

2	pounds medium shrimp, peeled and deveined
1	cup all-purpose flour
2	teaspoons salt
1	teaspoon baking powder
1/2	teaspoon ground red pepper
3/4	cup beer
1/2	cup milk
2	large eggs
	Oil for deep frying

With a paring knife, open each shrimp down the back without cutting all the way through to butterfly it, then press it flat.

In a bowl, combine the flour, salt, baking powder, and red pepper. Whisk in the beer, milk, and eggs. Add the shrimp to the batter and let stand for 30 minutes.

In a deep fryer, heat the oil to 365°. Remove the shrimp 1 at a time from the batter and fry them in small batches for 4 minutes total, turning twice, to ensure they are golden brown and crispy. Remove the shrimp to paper towels to drain. Serve the Beer-Battered Shrimp with the Cocktail Sauce on page 131.

❧ DRUNKEN SHRIMP ❧

· Yields 4 Servings

2	pounds fresh shrimp in the shell
3	cups beer
1	clove garlic, chopped
1	teaspoon salt
1/2	teaspoon thyme
1	teaspoon celery seed
1	tablespoon minced parsley
	Few dashes of Tabasco sauce
2	teaspoons lemon juice
	Melted butter

In a saucepan, combine the shrimp, beer, garlic, salt, thyme, celery seed, parsley, Tabasco sauce, and lemon juice. Bring the mixture to a boil. Simmer for about 4 minutes or until the shrimp are pink. Drain the shrimp. Serve the shrimp with the melted butter.

"In Heaven there is no beer
(No beer?!)
That's why we drink it here
And when we're all gone from here
Our friends will be drinking all the beer."

"In Heaven There Is No Beer"

❊⧼ SHRIMP WITH YOGURT DIP ⧽❊

· Yields 2 Servings

For the Shrimp:

12	ounces light beer
1	tablespoon onion flakes
4	peppercorns
1	bay leaf
1	whole clove
24	small shrimp, peeled and deveined

In a saucepan, combine the light beer, onion flakes, peppercorns, bay leaf, and clove. Bring the mixture to a boil and cook for 5 minutes. Add the shrimp, remove the pan from the heat, and let stand for 3 to 5 minutes until the shrimp turns pink. Drain. Cover the shrimp and chill.

For the Yogurt Dip:

1/2	cup plain unflavored yogurt
1	tablespoon + 1 teaspoon mayonnaise
1	tablespoon + 1 teaspoon chili sauce
1	teaspoon horseradish
1	teaspoon chopped capers
1/4	teaspoon Worcestershire sauce
2	to 3 drops hot pepper sauce

In a bowl, combine all of the ingredients for the dip. Mix the ingredients well and serve with the shrimp.

❧ COCONUT-FRIED SHRIMP ❧

· Yields 4 Servings

12	ounces light beer
2	cups all-purpose flour
3	teaspoons kosher salt
3	teaspoons sweet paprika
2	cups shredded unsweetened coconut
1	pound shrimp with tail, deveined
	Oil for deep frying

In a bowl, combine the light beer, flour, salt, and paprika to create the batter. Stir 1¼ cups of the coconut into the batter. Add the shrimp and stir to coat.

Place the remaining coconut on a plate. Remove the shrimp from the batter and coat with the coconut.

Heat the oil in a deep fryer to 325°. Deep fry the shrimp, in batches, for about 40 seconds per batch until they are golden brown.

"OH, LAGER BEER! IT MAKES GOOD CHEER, AND PROVES THE POOR MAN'S WORTH; IT COOLS THE BODY THROUGH AND THROUGH, AND REGULATES THE HEALTH."

Anonymous

❧ DILL POACHED SHRIMP ❧

· Yields 4 Servings

12	ounces light beer
5	dill sprigs
3	cloves garlic, peeled and diced
1	bay leaf
¼	teaspoon dried thyme
⅛	teaspoon cayenne pepper
	Salt and freshly ground black pepper to taste
1	pound medium shrimp, peeled and deveined

In a pot, combine the light beer, dill sprigs, garlic, bay leaf, thyme, cayenne pepper, salt, and black pepper. Bring the mixture to a boil. Lower the heat and simmer, covered, for 10 minutes. Add the shrimp, return to a boil, and simmer for 30 seconds. Remove the shrimp from the pot and drain.

❧ HERBED SHRIMP ❧

· Yields 6 Servings

2	pounds shrimp, peeled and deveined
1½	cups beer
2	cloves garlic, minced
2	tablespoons snipped fresh chives
2	tablespoons snipped fresh parsley
1½	teaspoons salt
½	teaspoon pepper
	Shredded lettuce
2	green onions, chopped

In a medium bowl, combine the shrimp, beer, garlic, chives, parsley, salt, and pepper, mixing well. Cover and refrigerate the mixture for 8 hours.

Drain the shrimp and reserve the marinade. Broil the shrimp approximately 4-inches from the heat until they are tender, brushing them with the reserved marinade. Garnish each serving with the lettuce and green onions.

⁂{ GARLIC SHRIMP }⁂

· Yields 12 Servings

2	teaspoons minced garlic
1	teaspoon dried oregano
1	teaspoon dried basil
1	teaspoon dried thyme
1	teaspoon cayenne pepper
1/2	teaspoon crushed red pepper flakes
1/2	teaspoon salt (or to taste)
1/2	teaspoon pepper (or to taste)
4	tablespoons butter
2	pounds shrimp, peeled and deveined
1/2	cup beer

In a skillet, combine the garlic, oregano, basil, thyme, cayenne pepper, red paper flakes, salt, pepper, and butter, sautéing the mixture until the garlic is lightly browned. Add the shrimp, stirring until the shrimp turn pink. Pour in the beer and simmer the mixture, uncovered, for 1 minute.

❧ LEEKS & SHRIMP ❧

· Yields 4 to 6 Servings

24	ounces beer
3	leeks, chopped
2	onions, chopped
3	sprigs parsley
1	bay leaf
1	rib celery
6	tablespoons butter
3	tablespoons all-purpose flour
2	pounds shrimp, peeled and deveined
	Salt and pepper to taste

In a saucepan, combine the beer, leeks, onions, parsley, bay leaf, and celery, mixing well. Simmer the mixture, uncovered, for 15 minutes.

Strain out the vegetables and discard the bay leaf. In a skillet, melt the butter and add the flour. Add the strained beer, stirring until the mixture is thickened. Add the shrimp and simmer, uncovered, for 5 minutes until the shrimp turn pink, seasoning with the salt and pepper to taste.

Serve the shrimp with the vegetables.

"No soldier can fight unless he is properly fed on beef and beer."
John Churchill, First Duke of Marlborough

❧ SOFTSHELL CRABS ❧

· Yields 6 Servings

12	ounces beer
1¼	cups all-purpose flour (plus extra for dusting)
2	teaspoons salt
1	teaspoon paprika
½	teaspoon baking powder
12	softshell crabs
	Oil for deep frying

In a medium bowl, combine all of the ingredients, except the softshell crabs, mixing well. Let the batter stand for at least 1½ hours, allowing it to thicken.

Dust the softshell crabs with the flour and completely coat them with the batter. In a deep fryer, fry the softshell crabs at 360° for 2 to 5 minutes, depending on their size, until they are golden. Drain the softshell crabs on paper towels.

❧ LOBSTER TAIL ❧

· Yields 2 Servings

12	ounces beer
2	whole lobster tails, thawed and out of the shell or split the shell lengthwise
	Warm melted butter or Cocktail Sauce (page 131)

In a medium saucepan, bring the beer to a boil over a medium to high heat. Place the lobster tails in a steamer basket on top of the saucepan and cover the basket. Reduce the heat and simmer the lobster tails for 8 minutes or until desired doneness. Serve the lobster tails with the melted butter or Cocktail Sauce.

☼⟩ OYSTERS ⟨☼

· Yields 6 Servings

1	cup self-rising flour (plus extra for coating)
	Pinch of salt
½	cup beer
½	cup water
24	to 36 fresh oysters
¼	cup chopped fresh dill
	Oil for deep frying

In a medium bowl, sift the flour and salt together. Make a well in the middle of the flour. Pour the beer followed by the water into the flour, mixing well to create a thick and smooth batter.

In a plastic bag, toss the oysters in the dill and then lightly coat each oyster with flour.

In a deep fryer, fry the oysters at 350° for approximately 2 minutes or until the oysters rise to the top and are golden. Drain the oysters on paper towels and pat them dry.

Serve the Oysters with the Cocktail Sauce on page 131 or your favorite sauce of choice.

"IF YOU EVER REACH TOTAL ENLIGHTENMENT
WHILE DRINKING BEER, I BET IT MAKES BEER
SHOOT OUT YOUR NOSE."

Jack Handey, American Humorist

❧ SCALLOPS ❧

· Yields 6 Servings

1	cup self-rising flour, divided
1/4	cup self-rising yellow cornmeal
5	dashes hot sauce
	Salt and pepper to taste
12	ounces beer
1/2	pound bay scallops, rinsed and drained
	Oil for deep frying

In a large bowl, combine half of the flour, cornmeal, hot sauce, salt, and pepper with enough beer to make the batter a little thinner than pancake batter.

In a plastic bag, shake the scallops and the remaining flour together, completely coating the scallops. Completely coat the scallops with the beer batter.

In a deep fryer, fry the scallops at 350° until they are golden. Drain the scallops on paper towels and pat them dry.

"I AM A FIRM BELIEVER IN THE PEOPLE. IF GIVEN THE TRUTH, THEY CAN BE DEPENDED UPON TO MEET ANY NATIONAL CRISIS. THE GREAT POINT IS TO BRING THEM THE REAL FACTS, AND BEER."

Abraham Lincoln, 16th U.S. President

❧ MUSSELS ❧

· Yields 4 to 6 Servings

6	to 7 pounds mussels, washed, bearded, and shells scrubbed (discard any open mussels)
1	carrot, sliced
1	leek, sliced
1	onion, diced
1	red pepper, chopped
¼	cup beer
11	black peppercorns
½	teaspoon salt
1	bay leaf
	Old Bay Seasoning to taste (optional)

Place the mussels in cold water until you are ready to use them.

In a large pot, combine all of the other ingredients. Bring the ingredients to a boil. Add the mussels and cook them for about 5 to 10 minutes. Continue to stir the mixture, cooking until the mussel shells are all open. With a slotted spoon, remove the mussels from the pot and serve.

"WHO DOES NOT LOVE BEER, WINE, WOMEN AND SONG remains a FOOL HIS WHOLE LIFE LONG."

Carl Worner, American actor and singer

❧ CLAMS ❧

· Yields 2 to 4 Servings

2	dozen fresh clams (should be tightly closed before cooking)
2	tablespoons cornmeal
1	cup water
½	cup beer
¼	teaspoon crushed dried thyme
1	small onion, chopped
	Melted butter

Scrub the clams with a brush under cold running water. Place the clams into a large bowl. Sprinkle the clams with the cornmeal and cover with cold water. Let the clams stand in a cool place for 1 to 2 hours. Drain the clams.

In a kettle, combine the 1 cup of water, beer, thyme, and onion. Add the clams. Cover and place over a high heat. Boil hard until the clams open. Check after 3 or 4 minutes and remove any clams that have opened. Discard any clams that have not opened after 15 minutes. Pour the pan broth over the clams in serving bowls. Serve the clams with the melted butter.

"We old folks have to find our cushions and pillows in our tankards.
Strong beer is the milk of the old."

Martin Luther, German monk, theologian, and church reformer

❖{ CALAMARI }❖

· Yields 4 Servings

2½	pounds calamari (squid)
1½	cups rye flour
1	tablespoon peanut oil
	Salt and freshly ground pepper to taste
24	ounces beer
5	egg whites, beaten until stiff but not dry
	Oil for deep frying
2	bunches curly parsley

To clean the squid, remove the purplish skin and separate the head and tentacles from the body. Remove and discard the transparent quill from the body. Wash out the interior of the body. Dry the body with paper towels. Cut the body into ½-inch wide rings. Leave the tentacles uncut.

In a bowl, whisk to combine the rye flour, peanut oil, salt, and pepper. Whisk in the beer a little at a time. Fold in the egg whites.

In a deep fryer, heat the oil to 375°. Dip the squid rings and tentacles into the batter and then fry them in the oil for 2½ minutes. Drain the squid on paper towels. Keep them warm.

Dry the parsley well and submerge it in the oil for 20 seconds. Drain the parsley on paper towels. Arrange the calamari in a ring on a large platter and top it with the parsley.

"I INTRODUCED ELIZABETH TO BEER, SHE INTRODUCED ME TO BULGARI."

Richard Burton, American actor

CHAPTER 18

Pasta

❧ CHICKEN & SPAGHETTI ❧

· Yields 6 Servings

12	ounces spaghetti, cooked and kept warm
1	tablespoon unsalted butter
2	tablespoons bacon drippings
1	large onion, chopped
3	celery ribs, chopped
1	green bell pepper, chopped
1	cup minced mushrooms
3	cloves garlic, minced
1	teaspoon Worcestershire sauce
2	teaspoons chili powder
1	tablespoon all-purpose flour
1½	cups beer
3	ripe tomatoes
¼	cup chili sauce
¾	cup half and half
2	tablespoons minced parsley
2	cups diced chicken
½	cup sliced green olives
2	cups grated Cheddar cheese

Preheat the oven to 350°. In a medium bowl, combine the spaghetti and butter, tossing to mix. In a skillet over a medium heat, warm the bacon drippings. Add the onion, celery, pepper, mushrooms, garlic, Worcestershire sauce, and chili powder, stirring for about 15 minutes until the vegetables are tender.

Sprinkle the flour over the vegetable mixture, stirring to mix. Add the beer, tomatoes, and chili sauce. Bring the mixture to a boil, reduce the heat, and simmer the mixture, uncovered, for approximately 30 minutes until the sauce is thick.

Remove the skillet from the heat and add the half and half and parsley, mixing well. Pour the sauce over the spaghetti and mix well.

In a casserole dish, layer half of the spaghetti. Top with half each of the chicken, olives, and Cheddar cheese. Place another spaghetti layer on top of the chicken layer. Finally, layer with the remaining chicken, olives, and cheese. Bake the Chicken & Spaghetti at 350° for approximately 25 minutes or until the cheese melts.

"YOU CAN'T BE A REAL COUNTRY UNLESS YOU HAVE A BEER AND AN AIRLINE—IT HELPS IF YOU HAVE SOME KIND OF A FOOT-BALL TEAM, OR SOME NUCLEAR WEAPONS, BUT AT THE VERY LEAST YOU NEED A BEER."

Frank Zappa, American singer

⁘{ SHRIMP & PASTA }⁘

· Yields 1 Serving

12	ounces beer
1	pound shrimp, peeled and deveined
1	cup vertically sliced onion
1½	teaspoons grated lemon rind
½	teaspoon salt
¼	teaspoon pepper
1	clove garlic, minced
2	tablespoons extra virgin olive oil
2	tablespoons lemon juice
4	cups angel hair pasta, cooked and kept warm
	Minced parsley to taste

In a Dutch oven, boil the beer. Add the shrimp and cook the mixture, covered, for 2 minutes over a high heat. Remove the shrimp and set them aside. Add the onion, lemon rind, salt, pepper, and garlic to the Dutch oven and bring the mixture to a boil. Cook the mixture, uncovered, for 4 minutes.

Remove the mixture from the heat. Add the extra virgin olive oil and lemon juice, stirring the mixture. Add the pasta, mixing well.

Top each serving of pasta with the shrimp and garnish with the parsley.

❧ CHEESE SAUCE & PASTA ❧

· Yields 4 Servings

2	medium carrots, sliced
1	small zucchini, chopped
1	cup quartered fresh mushrooms
2	tablespoons butter
2	tablespoons all-purpose flour
1	cup milk
¼	cup beer
¾	cup shredded Cheddar cheese
	Salt and pepper to taste
8	ounces tri-colored corkscrew pasta, cooked and kept warm

In a medium saucepan, combine the carrots, zucchini, mushrooms, and butter, mixing well. Sauté the mixture until the vegetables are tender.

Stir in the flour. Add the milk. Continue to cook and stir the mixture until it is thickened and bubbly and then cook it for 1 more minute.

Add the beer, mixing well, and heat the mixture thoroughly.

Remove the mixture from the heat. Add the Cheddar cheese, mixing well until the cheese is melted. Add the salt and pepper to taste. Pour the cheese sauce over each serving of pasta.

"[I recommend]… bread, meat, vegetables and beer."

Sophocles, Greek tragedian, Sophocles' philosophy of a moderate diet

❧ EGGPLANT & PASTA ❧

· Yields 4 to 6 Servings

½	cup olive oil
1	medium eggplant, peeled and diced
	Salt and pepper to taste
6	ounces smoked ham, cubed
1	cup beer
½	teaspoon dried rosemary
1	cup frozen peas
1	pound penne pasta, cooked and kept warm
	Grated Parmesan cheese

In a skillet, heat the olive oil over a medium heat. Add the eggplant and season with the salt and pepper to taste, stirring and cooking for approximately 8 to 10 minutes or until the eggplant becomes tender.

Stir in the ham, frying it for 2 minutes. Add the beer and rosemary, bringing the mixture to a boil until the liquid is reduced by half.

Add the peas and simmer the mixture, covered, for 2 minutes. Stir in the pasta, cooking for approximately 30 seconds or until the pasta is thoroughly cooked. Garnish each serving with the Parmesan cheese.

"FERMENTATION MAY HAVE BEEN A GREATER DISCOVERY THAN FIRE."

David Rains Wallace, American naturalist and author

❉⟩ BRATWURST & PASTA ⟨❉

· Yields 4 Servings

1	large red pepper, chopped
2	sweet onions, chopped
4	cloves garlic, chopped
1	tablespoon olive oil
15	ounces bratwurst
½	cup beer
½	cup fresh basil
1	pound rigatoni pasta, cooked and kept warm (reserve ½ cup of pasta water)
1½	cups shredded Cheddar cheese

Preheat the oven to 425°. In a casserole dish, combine the red peppers, onions, garlic, and olive oil, mixing well. Roast the mixture for 25 minutes, stirring occasionally.

In a skillet, remove the bratwurst casings, crumble the meat, and sauté it over a medium heat until it is well-browned.

Strain the fat from the skillet. With only the meat in the skillet, add the beer, cover, and simmer the mixture.

In the casserole dish, combine the meat and the vegetable mixture along with the basil, pasta, and 1 cup of the Cheddar cheese, mixing well. If the mixture appears dry, add some of the reserved pasta water. Garnish each serving with the remaining Cheddar cheese.

❧ SMOKED SAUSAGE & PASTA ❧

· Yields 6 Servings

1	pound smoked sausage, cut into 1-inch pieces
1	cup sliced fresh mushrooms
2	ribs celery, sliced
1	large green bell pepper, cut into 1-inch pieces
1	medium onion, chopped
1	cup beer
1	8-ounce can tomato sauce
½	cup water
2	tablespoons snipped parsley
½	teaspoon sugar
½	teaspoon caraway seeds
4	ounces spaghetti, broken into 2-inch pieces and cooked
	Grated Parmesan cheese

In a Dutch oven, cook the smoked sausage until it is light brown. Remove the smoked sausage from the Dutch oven and set it aside.

In the Dutch oven, combine the mushrooms, celery, pepper, and onion, mixing well. Cook the mixture, uncovered, for approximately 3 minutes or until the vegetables are tender.

Drain the fat from the Dutch oven. Stir in the beer, tomato sauce, water, parsley, sugar, and caraway seeds, mixing well. Bring the mixture to a boil. Reduce the heat and simmer the mixture, covered, for 20 minutes.

Stir in the spaghetti and bring the mixture to a boil. Reduce the heat and simmer the mixture, covered, for 12 minutes or until the spaghetti is tender.

Add the smoked sausage and cook through. Garnish each serving with the Parmesan cheese.

CHAPTER 19

Cakes

❊❳ GOLDEN CHEESECAKE ❳❊

· Yields 12 Servings

¾	cup all-purpose flour
3	tablespoons sugar
1½	teaspoons lemon zest
6	tablespoons butter
3	egg yolks, beaten
¼	teaspoon vanilla extract
24	ounces cream cheese, softened
1½	cups shredded Cheddar cheese, room temperature
1¼	cups sugar
2	tablespoons cornstarch
2	teaspoons orange peel
3	eggs
⅔	cup milk
¼	cup beer

In a large bowl, combine the flour, sugar, and ½ teaspoon of the lemon zest. Cut in the butter. Stir in 1 egg yolk and the vanilla. Pat two thirds of the dough onto the bottom of a springform pan without the sides attached. Bake in a 400° oven for 8 to 9 minutes or until golden. Cool.

Butter the sides of the pan and attach them to the bottom. Pat the remaining dough 1¾ inches up the pan sides. Increase the oven temperature to 450°.

In a second bowl, beat the cream cheese until it is creamy. Add the Cheddar cheese. Beat the mixture until no yellow specks are visible.

In a third bowl, combine the sugar and cornstarch, and add to the cheese along with the orange peel and remaining 1 teaspoon of lemon zest. Mix well. Add the eggs and remaining 2 egg yolks. Mix until blended well. Stir in the milk and beer and then pour into the crust. Bake in a 450° oven for 10 minutes. Reduce the temperature to 300° and bake for 55 to 60 more minutes or until the center appears to be set. Remove the cake from the oven. Cool for 15 minutes.

Loosen the sides of the cheesecake from the pan with a spatula. Cool the cake for 30 minutes. Remove the sides of the pan. Cool the cake for 2 hours and then serve.

❧ GINGERSNAP CHEESECAKE ❧

· Yields 16 Servings

1¼	cups gingersnap cookie crumbs (from approximately 20 cookies)
2	tablespoons sugar
1	teaspoon ground ginger
¼	cup (½ stick) unsalted butter
24	ounces cream cheese, softened
1	cup shredded sharp Cheddar cheese
1	cup sugar
5	large eggs, room temperature
¼	cup beer
¼	cup heavy cream

Preheat the oven to 300°. In a medium bowl, combine the gingersnap crumbs, the 2 tablespoons of sugar, ginger, and butter, mixing well. Firmly press this mixture into the bottom of a 9-inch buttered spring form pan with removable sides. Chill the mixture in the pan.

In a large bowl, combine the cream cheese and Cheddar cheese, beating the mixture until it is smooth. Slowly add the 1 cup of sugar, beating the mixture until it is light and fluffy. Add the eggs, one at a time, beating until each one is mixed in. Slowly beat in the beer and heavy cream. Pour this batter into the chilled pan. Bake the batter at 325° for 1½ hours or until the center is set and the top is golden.

Crack open the oven door and let the cake set for 30 minutes. Place the cake on a rack to cool. Chill the Gingersnap Cheesecake for several hours to overnight before serving.

❧ STACK CAKE ❧

1	cup (2 sticks) butter
1	cup sugar
1	cup molasses
3	eggs
4	cups all-purpose flour
1	teaspoon baking soda
1	teaspoon salt
1	cup beer
30	ounces chunky-style applesauce
1/2	teaspoon ground cinnamon
	Whipped cream
	Sliced apples

Grease and flour 3 8-inch round pans.

In a large bowl, cream the butter and sugar until the mixture is light and fluffy. Beat in the molasses. Add the eggs, one at a time. Beat well after adding each egg.

In a small bowl, combine the flour, baking soda, and salt. Add this mixture to the creamed mixture alternately with the beer, beating after each addition.

Pour 1½ cups of the batter into the prepared pans. Refrigerate the remaining batter. Bake in a 375° oven for about 15 minutes or until the cakes test done. Cool the cakes in the pans for 5 minutes. Remove the cakes from the pans and cool on wire racks.

Wash the pans and grease and flour them again. Repeat the baking with the remaining batter.

In a medium bowl, combine the applesauce and cinnamon. Spread this mixture between the cooled cake layers. Spread the whipped cream on top. Garnish with the sliced apples.

❧ SPICE CAKE ❧

· Yields 6 to 8 Servings

2/3	cup (11 tablespoons) butter
1½	cups firmly packed brown sugar
2	eggs
2½	cups all-purpose flour
1½	teaspoons baking powder
½	teaspoon baking soda
¼	teaspoon salt
1	teaspoon ground cinnamon
1	teaspoon ground allspice
12	ounces beer
½	cup walnuts
½	cup golden raisins

In a medium bowl, combine the butter and brown sugar, creaming the mixture well. Beat in the eggs, one at a time, blending well.

In another medium bowl, combine the flour, baking powder, baking soda, salt, cinnamon, and allspice, mixing well. Add the flour mixture to the egg mixture along with the beer, mixing well. Stir in the walnuts and raisins, mixing well. Pour the mixture into a tube pan. Bake at 350° for 1 hour or until a knife inserted into the cake comes out clean.

Leave the cake in the pan to cool for 10 minutes and then remove the cake and place it on a rack to further cool.

Top the cake with ice cream or your favorite frosting.

❧{ COCOA CAKE }☙

· Yields 6 to 8 Servings

2	cups sugar
3	cups all-purpose flour
½	cup cocoa
1	teaspoon salt
2	teaspoons baking soda
¾	cup oil
4	teaspoons vinegar
1	teaspoon vanilla extract
12	ounces beer
½	cup water

In a bowl, sift the sugar, flour, cocoa, salt, and baking soda together. Make 1 large and 2 small wells in the dry mixture. Pour the oil into the large well. Pour the vinegar into the first small well. Pour the vanilla into the second small well. Pour the beer over all. Add the water. Stir the mixture well. Place the mixture in a baking pan and bake at 350° for 25 to 30 minutes.

"... there is only one game at the heart of America and that is baseball, and only one beverage to be found sloshing at the depths of our national soul and that is beer."

Peter Richmond, American author

❈} CHOCOLATE CHIP & WALNUT CAKE }❈

· Yields 8 Servings

¾	cup (1½ sticks) butter
1½	cups sugar
3	eggs
1½	teaspoons vanilla extract
2	cups sour cream
3	cups all-purpose flour
½	teaspoon baking powder
1½	teaspoons baking soda
⅛	teaspoon salt
¾	cup beer
¾	cup chopped walnuts
¾	cup chocolate chips
½	cup sugar
4	tablespoons ground cinnamon

In a medium bowl, combine the butter and sugar, creaming the mixture until it is fluffy. Add the eggs, one at a time, blending the mixture well. Add the vanilla and sour cream, blending the mixture well until it is creamy. Add the flour, baking powder, baking soda, salt, and beer, blending the mixture well.

In a small bowl, combine the walnuts, chocolate chips, sugar, and cinnamon. Add the walnut mixture to the flour mixture, mixing well. Pour the mixture into a greased and floured tube pan. Bake the mixture at 350° for approximately 1 hour or until a knife inserted into the cake comes out clean.

Leave the cake in the pan to cool for 10 minutes and then remove the cake and place it on a rack to further cool.

Leave the cake plain or top it with your favorite frosting.

⁎⟩ HONEY CAKE ⟨⁎

· Yields 10 Servings

½	cup (1 stick) butter
2	cups sugar
4	eggs
½	cup orange juice
½	cup apple butter
¾	cup honey
4	cups sifted all-purpose flour
2	teaspoons baking powder
¼	teaspoon salt
1	teaspoon baking soda
1	teaspoon grated nutmeg
1	teaspoon ground cloves
1	teaspoon ground cinnamon
1	teaspoon ground allspice
1	cup beer
1	cup seedless raisins, coated with flour
½	cup chopped black walnuts, coated with flour
	Confectioners' sugar

Preheat the oven to 325°. In a medium bowl, combine the butter and sugar, creaming the mixture until it is fluffy. Add the eggs, one at a time, beating the mixture until it is creamy. Add the orange juice, apple butter, and honey, mixing well.

In a small bowl, combine the flour, baking powder, salt, baking soda, nutmeg, cloves, cinnamon, and allspice, mixing well. Alternately add the flour mixture and the beer to the egg mixture, beginning and ending with the flour mixture. Add the raisins and walnuts, mixing well. Pour the mixture into a greased and floured tube pan. Bake the mixture at 325° for 1 hour and 20 minutes.

Top the cake with a dusting of confectioners' sugar.

❈{ DOUBLE CHOCOLATE CAKE }❈

· Yields 6 to 8 Servings

For the Cake:

⅓	cup (5 tablespoons plus 1 teaspoon) butter
1	cup sugar
2	egg yolks
2	squares unsweetened chocolate, melted and cooled
¾	cup cold beer
1¾	cups all-purpose flour
1	teaspoon baking powder
¼	teaspoon baking soda
½	teaspoon salt

In a medium bowl, cream together the butter and sugar. Add the egg yolks, one at a time, beating until it is well-blended. Add the chocolate, beating the mixture until it is smooth. Add the beer followed by the flour, baking powder, baking soda, and salt, beating until smooth. Pour the batter into a greased tube pan. Bake at 375° for 30 minutes.

For the Frosting:

½	cup cocoa
1⅓	cups sugar
5	tablespoons cornstarch
¼	teaspoon salt
1½	cups milk
1	teaspoon butter
1	teaspoon vanilla extract

In a saucepan, combine the cocoa, sugar, cornstarch, and salt, mixing well. Add the milk, mixing well. Cook the frosting mixture over a medium heat while constantly stirring until the mixture is thickened. When the frosting mixture is finished on the stove, remove it, and add the butter and vanilla, mixing well. Top the cake with the frosting.

❧ TWIN FUDGE CAKES ❧

²⁄₃	cup (10 tablespoons plus 2 teaspoons) butter
1½	cups sugar
3	eggs
1	teaspoon vanilla extract
½	cup cocoa
2¼	cups sifted all-purpose flour
1	teaspoon baking powder
1	teaspoon baking soda
	Salt to taste
1	cup beer
²⁄₃	cup sauerkraut
1	cup raisins
1	cup chopped walnuts

In a medium bowl, combine the butter and sugar, creaming the mixture until it is smooth. Add the eggs, one at a time, beating the mixture well. Add the vanilla, blending well.

In a small bowl, sift together the cocoa, flour, baking powder, baking soda, and salt to taste. Alternately add the cocoa mixture and beer to the butter mixture, beginning and ending with the cocoa mixture. Stir in the sauerkraut, raisins, and walnuts. Pour the batter into 2 greased and floured cake pans. Bake at 350° for 35 minutes.

Place the cakes on a rack to cool. Top the cakes with your favorite frosting.

❖{ VANILLA & CINNAMON CAKE }❖

· Yields 6 to 8 Servings

³/₄	cup (1¹/₂ sticks) butter
1¹/₂	cups sugar
3	cups all-purpose flour
1¹/₂	teaspoons baking powder
1¹/₂	teaspoons baking soda
¹/₂	teaspoon salt
3	eggs
1¹/₂	cups sour cream
1¹/₂	teaspoons vanilla extract
¹/₂	cup beer
¹/₂	cup sugar
2	teaspoons ground cinnamon
²/₃	cup chopped walnuts or dates

In a medium bowl, combine the butter and the 1¹/₂ cups of sugar, creaming the mixture until it is smooth.

In another medium bowl, combine the flour, baking powder, baking soda, salt, eggs, sour cream, and vanilla, mixing well. Alternately add the flour mixture and the beer to the butter mixture, mixing well. Pour the batter into a greased tube pan.

In a small bowl, combine the ¹/₂ cup of sugar, cinnamon, and walnuts, mixing well. This will create the topping. Sprinkle one third of the topping mixture on the batter. Bake at 350° for approximately 45 to 50 minutes.

Place the Vanilla & Cinnamon Cake on a rack to cool and dust the top with the remaining topping mixture.

⁖{ EASY VANILLA CAKE }⁖

· Yields 6 to 8 Servings

1	18.25-ounce package white cake mix
1	3-ounce package vanilla instant pudding
1	cup beer
¼	cup liquid shortening
4	eggs

In a large bowl, combine the white cake mix and vanilla instant pudding, mixing well. Add the beer and liquid shortening, mixing lightly. Add the eggs, beating the mixture until it is creamy and thick. Pour the batter into a greased tube pan. Bake at 350° for approximately 1 hour.

Place the cake on a rack to cool. Top the cake with your favorite vanilla frosting.

⁖{ ST. PATRICK'S DAY CAKE }⁖

· Yields 6 to 8 Servings

½	cup (1 stick) butter
1	cup firmly packed brown sugar
3	eggs, beaten
2¼	cups self-rising flour
	Pinch of salt
½	teaspoon apple pie spice
⅔	cup raisins (soaked in beer overnight)
½	cup candied peel (soaked)
1⅓	cup golden raisins (soaked)
¼	cup candied cherries
8	ounces beer

Preheat the oven to 350°. In a medium bowl, combine the butter and brown sugar, creaming the mixture until it is mixed well. Beat in the eggs, one at a time, blending until the mixture is smooth. Add the flour, salt, apple pie spice, raisins, candied peel, golden raisins, and candied cherries, mixing well. Add the beer, mixing well. Pour the batter into a greased cake pan. Bake for approximately 2 hours, until the center is firm.

ᵈ❦ CHERRY CAKE ❦ᵈ

· Yields 10 Servings

4	eggs
2	cups sugar
2	teaspoons vanilla extract
2	cups sifted all-purpose flour
2	teaspoons baking powder
1/4	teaspoon salt
1	cup beer
2	tablespoons butter, melted
1	cup maraschino cherries

Preheat the oven to 375°. In a medium bowl, beat the eggs until they are thickened. Beat in the sugar. Add the vanilla, mixing well. Fold the flour, baking powder, and salt into the egg mixture.

In a saucepan, heat the beer. Add the beer and butter to the batter. Line a greased tube pan with the maraschino cherries. Pour the batter into the tube pan. Bake at 375° for 30 minutes.

Remove the cake from the tube pan and place it on a rack to cool.

Top the cake with more maraschino cherries or your favorite frosting.

❧ HOLIDAY FRUITCAKE ❧

· Yields 24 Servings

24	ounces beer
2	cups raisins
8	ounces pitted dates, snipped
1	cup chopped dried apples
1	cup chopped dried apricots
4	cups all-purpose flour
1½	cups firmly packed brown sugar
1	teaspoon ground cinnamon
½	teaspoon ground allspice
½	teaspoon ground cloves
1	teaspoon baking soda
1¼	cups (2½ sticks) butter
4	eggs
1	teaspoon grated lemon peel
1	cup chopped walnuts

In a saucepan, bring 12 ounces of the beer to a boil. Remove it from the heat. Add the raisins, dates, apples, and apricots and let the mixture stand for 1 hour, occasionally stirring it.

In a medium bowl, combine the flour, brown sugar, cinnamon, allspice, cloves, and baking soda, mixing well. Cut in the butter until the mixture has the appearance of small peas.

In another medium bowl, combine the eggs, the remaining 12 ounces of beer, and lemon peel. Add the egg mixture to the flour mixture, mixing well. Drain the fruit mixture, reserving the juice. Fold the fruit mixture and walnuts into the main batter. Pour the batter into a greased and floured tube pan. Bake at 350° for approximately 2 hours or until the cake tests done.

Remove the cake from the pan and cool completely. Soak a cheesecloth in the reserved juice and then wrap the cake in the cheesecloth. Add additional beer, if necessary, for moistness. Tightly wrap the cake in aluminum foil. Store the Holiday Fruitcake in a cool place for approximately 1 week before serving. You can remoisten the cheesecloth with more beer if needed.

CHAPTER 20

Cookies, Pastries, & Ice Cream

❧ CINNAMON & WALNUT COOKIES ❧

· Yields 40 Cookies

½	cup (1 stick) butter
½	cup firmly packed brown sugar
2	cups all-purpose flour
½	teaspoon baking soda
1	teaspoon ground cinnamon
1¼	cups beer (room temperature)
½	cup walnuts

In a medium bowl, combine the butter and brown sugar, creaming the mixture until it is smooth. Cut in the flour, baking soda, and cinnamon. Slowly blend in the beer, creating a soft dough. Drop teaspoon-size amounts of the batter onto a cookie sheet. Place 1 walnut on each mound of batter. Bake at 350° for 20 minutes until the cookies are lightly browned.

Cool the Cinnamon & Walnut Cookies for 1 minute on the cookie sheet and then transfer the cookies to a rack to completely cool.

"I'M GOING TO BUY A BOAT... DO A LITTLE TRAVELLING, AND I'M GOING TO BE DRINKING BEER!"

John Welsh, Brooklyn bus driver who won $30 million in the New York lottery

·}{ DEEP FRIED SUGAR COOKIES }{·

· Yields 40 Cookies

3	cups all-purpose flour
3	tablespoons sugar
½	cup (1 stick) butter
1	cup beer
	Oil for deep frying

In a medium bowl, combine the flour and sugar, mixing well. Cut in the butter. Stir in the beer, mixing well to form a thick batter. Shape the batter into a ball, invert a pan over the dough, and let it rise at room temperature for 30 minutes.

Roll the dough to approximately ¼-inch thick and then cut the dough into cookie-size pieces.

In a deep fryer, drop the individual cookies into the hot oil, cooking them until they are golden. Drain the Deep Fried Sugar Cookies on paper towels and cool before serving. Top them with your favorite frosting if desired.

"Give me a woman who loves beer and I will conquer the world."

Kaiser Wilhelm, German Emperor

❧ GREEK CHRISTMAS COOKIES ❧

· Yields 40 Cookies

For the Cookies:

1½	cups olive oil
½	cup (1 stick) unsalted butter (room temperature)
1	cup beer
¾	teaspoon ground cinnamon
¼	teaspoon ground cloves
	Grated peel of 1 orange
1	cup sugar
6	cups all-purpose flour
½	teaspoon baking soda
½	teaspoon baking powder
1	teaspoon salt
2	cups finely ground semolina

In a medium bowl, combine the olive oil, butter, beer, cinnamon, cloves, orange peel, and sugar, beating until well-mixed.

In another medium bowl, sift 1 cup of the flour together with the baking soda, baking powder, and salt, blending the mixture well. Add the semolina, 1 cup at a time, to the mixture. Add enough of the remaining flour, 1 cup at a time, until a firm dough has formed. Use your hands to mix the dough well. Roll the dough into cylinders, 2-inches long and 1-inch in diameter, flatten the cylinders with your hand, and place them on a cookie sheet, which has been greased with a little olive oil. Bake the dough at 350° for 30 minutes.

Remove the cookies from the oven and let them cool for 30 minutes.

For the Syrup:

1½	cups sugar
1½	cups honey
1	cup water
½	cup chopped walnuts

In a saucepan, combine the sugar, honey, and water, mixing well. Bring the mixture to a boil. Reduce the heat and cook the syrup mixture, uncovered, for 3 minutes, skimming off the foam that forms on the top. Pour the hot syrup over the Greek Christmas Cookies and sprinkle them with the walnuts. Let the cookies soak overnight.

❧ PINEAPPLE COOKIE SQUARES ❧

· Yields 24 Squares

3	cups sifted all-purpose flour
5	teaspoons baking powder
1	cup shortening (Crisco)
	Pinch of salt
1	large egg, beaten
3/4	cup beer
2	16-ounce jars pineapple preserves
	Confectioners' sugar

In a medium bowl, combine the flour, baking powder, shortening, and salt, blending well.

In a small bowl, combine the egg and beer, mixing well. Add the egg mixture to the flour mixture, mixing well. Divide the dough into 3 equal parts and chill them for 1 hour. Roll each third of the dough out thin enough to fit on a cookie sheet. Layer the first piece of dough with 1 jar of the pineapple preserves. Place the next third of the dough on top of that. Layer the second jar of pineapple preserves on top of that piece of dough. Place the final third of the dough on top of that layer. Bake at 350° for 30 to 35 minutes.

While still warm, sprinkle the surface with the confectioners' sugar. Cut into cookie squares.

❧{ CHOCOLATE CANNOLI }☙

· Yields 9 Servings

For the Filling:

1	pound ricotta, drained
1	cup confectioners' sugar
½	cup toasted and chopped walnuts
⅓	cup semisweet chocolate chips
1	teaspoon grated orange peel
½	teaspoon grated lime peel

To create the filling, in a processor, combine the ricotta and sugar, puréeing the mixture until it is smooth. Transfer the mixture to a large bowl and add the walnuts, chocolate chips, orange peel, and lime peel, mixing well. Cover and refrigerate the filling until it is chilled.

Return the filling to room temperature before using it.

For the Cannoli Shells:

1	cup all-purpose flour
1	teaspoon baking powder
1	teaspoon confectioners' sugar
	Pinch of salt
⅓	cup beer
1	tablespoon unsalted butter, softened
1	egg, beaten and divided
1	teaspoon vanilla extract
	Oil

In a large bowl, combine the flour, baking powder, sugar, and salt. Make a well in the center of the mixture. Add the beer, butter, half of the egg, and vanilla. Draw the flour from the sides of the bowl until it is mixed well. Turn the dough out onto a floured board, kneading it until it is smooth. Cover the dough and let it stand for 1 hour.

Roll the dough out into a 12-inch square. Cut the square into 9 4-inch squares. Using cannoli forms, wrap 1 square around each cannoli form, brushing the edges with water and gently pressing the edges to seal.

Heat the oil in a deep fryer to 350°. Drop in the cannoli dough forms, cooking and turning them for approximately 4 minutes until they are golden. Drain the cannoli forms on paper towels and remove the cannoli shells from the forms.

Spoon the filling mixture into a pastry bag without the tip. Pipe the filling into the cannoli shells.

⁕} BUTTERSCOTCH TARTS {⁕

· Yields 6 Servings

1	3⅝-ounce package butterscotch pudding and pie filling
½	cup beer
1½	cups milk
1	teaspoon pumpkin pie spice (plus extra for dusting the tarts)
1	teaspoon instant coffee
6	baked tart shells
1	cup whipped cream

In a saucepan, cook the butterscotch pudding as directed, using the beer and milk for the liquids. When the pudding mixture thickens, add the pumpkin pie spice and instant coffee, mixing well. Cover the pudding and let it cool.

Beat the pudding mixture before using. Fill each tart with the pudding mixture and chill them until they are cold. Garnish each serving with the whipped cream and a dusting of the pumpkin pie spice.

❖⟨ CHOCOLATE MOUSSE ⟩❖

· Yields 6 to 8 Servings

1	pound chocolate chips
¾	cup beer (room temperature)
3	tablespoons coffee liqueur
8	large eggs, separated (room temperature
1¼	cups heavy whipping cream (chilled)
1	teaspoon vanilla extract
½	cup sugar
½	teaspoon cream of tartar

In a double broiler, melt the chocolate chips and then remove them from the heat. Stir in the beer and coffee liqueur, mixing until well-blended. Add the egg yolks, 2 at a time, blending well.

In a medium bowl, combine the whipping cream, vanilla, and sugar, whipping the mixture until it forms stiff peaks. Chill this mixture.

In another medium bowl, combine the egg whites and cream of tartar, whipping the mixture until it is stiff. Fold this mixture together with the whipping cream mixture. Slowly fold one fourth of this mixture into the chocolate chip mixture until the mixture is smooth. Fold in the remainder of the whipping cream mixture, mixing until no white is visible. Spoon the Chocolate Mousse into goblets or other serving dishes of choice and chill before serving.

"IT IS A FAIR WIND THAT BLEW MEN TO THE ALE."

Washington Irving, American author

❊{ ICE CREAM }❊

· Yields 2 Quarts

18	ounces beer
1	large egg
1	cup sugar
½	cup milk
2	cups heavy whipping cream

In a saucepan, boil the beer down to 1½ cups and then reduce the heat to low.

In a medium bowl, combine the egg and sugar, mixing well. Add the milk followed by the beer. Add the whipping cream, mixing well. Refrigerate the mixture for approximately 1 hour.

Pour the mixture into an ice cream maker and mix until desired doneness.

"Beer has long been the prime lubricant in our social intercourse and the sacred throat~anointing fluid that accompanies the ritual of mateship. To sink a few cold ones with the blokes is both an escape and a confirmation of belonging."

Rennie Ellis, Austrailian photographer

❧ FRIED ICE CREAM BALLS ❧

· Yields 8 Servings

8	balls ice cream (flavor of choice)
2	cups crushed cornflakes
1½	cups unbleached flour
1	tablespoon sugar
1	teaspoon salt
1	tablespoon vegetable oil
2	large egg yolks, lightly beaten
¾	cup flat beer
1	quart peanut oil
2	large egg whites

Make the batter a day before you plan to serve the ice cream.

Coat the ice cream balls with the crushed cornflakes the day before serving them and freeze them overnight.

In a medium bowl, combine the flour, sugar, salt, vegetable oil, and egg yolks, mixing well. Slowly stir in the beer. Refrigerate this mixture overnight.

In a deep fryer, heat the peanut oil to 375°. In a small bowl, beat the egg whites until they are stiff and fold them into the batter. Completely coat 3 of the ice cream balls at a time with the batter and drop them into the hot oil, frying them until they are golden. Remove the balls from the deep dryer and drain them on paper towels. Serve the Fried Ice Cream Balls immediately.

CHAPTER 21

Mixed Drinks

❧ SEVEN & LIME ❧

10	ounces beer
2	ounces 7-Up
½	teaspoon lime juice
	Crushed ice

Combine all ingredients, stirring well.

❧ BUZZY NAVEL ❧

⅓	ounce vodka
⅓	ounce peach schnapps
⅓	ounce beer
	Orange juice

Combine the vodka, peach schnapps, and beer on the rocks in a highball glass, stirring well. Fill the remainder of the glass with the orange juice.

❧ SNAKEBITE ❧

2	ounces beer
2	ounces apple cider
	Dash of raspberry liqueur
	Ice

Combine all ingredients in a shaker, shaking well, and then pour into a glass.

⁂{ LEMON JACK }⁂

1	ounce vodka
1	ounce Jack Daniel's Whiskey
1	ounce lemonade
1	ounce beer

Combine all ingredients on the rocks, stirring well.

⁂{ JUNGLE JUICE }⁂

1½	ounces white rum
1½	ounces gin
1½	ounces vodka
1	ounce triple sec
1½	ounces sour mix
1	teaspoon grenadine
1	teaspoon beer

Layer the ingredients in the above order over the rocks.

"LIFE ALAS, IS VERY DREAR. UP WITH THE GLASS, DOWN WITH THE BEER!"

Louis Untermeyer, American author

❖{ BEER BUSTER }❖

2	ounces vodka
12	ounces beer
	Dash of Tabasco sauce

Combine all ingredients on the rocks, stirring well.

❖{ DR. B }❖

1	ounce amaretto
1	ounce vodka
1	ounce Bacardi 151 Proof Rum
1	ounce Dr. Pepper
1	ounce beer

Combine the amaretto, vodka, and rum on the rocks. Stir in the Dr. Pepper and beer.

"A PINT OF GOOD BEER, IT'S EQUAVALENT TO
HALF A COLLEGE CREDIT IN PHILOSOPHY."

Raymond Hankins, American homebrewer

⁕{ HOOLA JUICE }⁕

	Pineapple juice (frozen into ice cubes)
12	ounces beer
4	tablespoons crushed pineapple
	Pineapple chunks
	Cherries

Place the pineapple ice cubes in a blender and crush. Pour the crushed pineapple ice into a glass. Add the beer, stirring well. Top with the crushed pineapple. Garnish by alternating the pineapple chunks and cherries on a pick and laying it across the top of the glass.

⁕{ ICED TEA }⁕

4	ounces unsweetened iced tea
	Sugar to taste
12	ounces beer
	Lemon slice
	Sprig of mint

Combine the iced tea and sugar on the rocks. Add the beer, stirring to mix and dissolve the sugar. Garnish with the lemon slice and sprig of mint.

❧ MALIBU RUMBLE ❧

5	ounces Bacardi 151 Black Bat Rum
2	ounces blue curacao
2	ounces Malibu Rum
	Splash of beer
	Crushed ice
	Mountain Dew

Combine all ingredients, except the Mountain Dew, in a tall glass, stirring well. Fill the remainder of the glass with the Mountain Dew.

❧ SUNRISE ❧

12	ounces beer
1	ounce amaretto
1	ounce orange juice
	Orange slice

Combine all ingredients on the rocks, stirring well. Garnish with the orange slice.

"LIFE'S TOO SHORT TO DRINK CHEAP BEER."

Anonymous

❊{ BEER BULLET }❊

2	ounces tequila
1	ounce Kahlua
1	ounce whiskey
1	ounce beer
1	ounce Mountain Dew

Combine all ingredients, stirring well.

❊{ ST. MARYS ROOT BEER }❊

1	ounce Galliano
1	ounce Kahlua
1	ounce cola
	Crushed ice
2½	ounces club soda
1	teaspoon beer

In a shaker, combine the Galliano, Kahlua, cola, and crushed ice, shaking well. Strain into a glass and add the club soda and beer. Serve on the rocks.

❖{ B-B-Q }❖

1	ounce Irish whiskey
2	ounces V-8 Juice
1	teaspoon barbecue sauce (smokey)
1	teaspoon lemon juice
	Beer
	Celery rib

Combine all ingredients, except the beer, in a highball glass. Fill the remainder of the glass with the beer. Garnish with the celery.

❖{ RED-HEADED MARY }❖

8	ounces tomato juice
	Splash of Tabasco sauce
	Splash of Worcestershire sauce
4	ounces beer
	Seasoned salt to taste
	Pepper to taste
	Celery rib

Layer the ingredients in the above order over the rocks, adding the seasoning to taste. Garnish with the celery.

⸗{ PEACH FIZZ }⸗

7	ounces peach schnapps
3	ounces beer
1	ounce Jack Daniel's Whiskey
3	ounces Slice
2	ounces lemonade
	Ice

Combine all ingredients in a shaker. Shake well and strain into a glass.

⸗{ COUNTRY LEMONADE }⸗

6	ounces gin
1	6-ounce can lemonade concentrate
12	ounces beer
	Water to taste (optional)
	Lemon slices

Combine all ingredients on the rocks in a pitcher, stirring well. Garnish with the lemon slices.

"What contemptible scoundrel has stolen the cork to my lunch?"

W.C. Fields, American comedian

❖{ BEER BLEEDER }❖

½	ounce vodka
½	ounce rum
½	ounce gin
½	ounce tequila
½	ounce triple sec
½	ounce brandy
½	ounce Malibu Rum
2	ounces beer
½	ounce lime juice
	Splash of grenadine

Combine all ingredients on the rocks, stirring well.

❖{ A BERRY SWEET }❖

1½	cups strawberries
1½	cups raspberries
1½	cups blueberries
1½	cups blackberries
2	lemons, squeezed
	Lemon juice
½	cup powdered sugar
	Crushed ice
3	12-ounce bottles beer

In a blender, combine all of the berries and reduce the mixture to juice. Add the juice from the 2 lemons, mixing well. Dip the rim of each frosted glass in the lemon juice and then the sugar. Fill each glass halfway with the crushed ice. Pour the berry-lemon juice mixture into the glasses, covering the ice. Fill the remainder of each glass with the beer.

ꙮ} BEER OVER CHERRY ROCKS {ꙮ

	Cherry 7-Up (frozen into ice cubes)
	Cherries (frozen inside the ice cubes)
12	ounces beer
2	ounces Cherry 7-Up

To make the cherry rocks, pour the Cherry 7-Up into an ice tray. Place one cherry in each ice tray cube and freeze. Fill a glass with the frozen cherry rocks and combine the beer and 2 ounces of Cherry 7-Up, stirring well.

ꙮ} GINGER ALE {ꙮ

6	ounces beer
6	ounces ginger ale
	Lemon slice
1	cherry

Combine the beer and ginger ale in a frosted glass, stirring well. Garnish with the lemon slice and cherry.

ꙮ} V BEER {ꙮ

| 2 | ounces Absolut Vanilla Vodka |
| 12 | ounces beer |

Combine both ingredients on the rocks, stirring well.

❧ A BEER SOUR ❧

½   ounce fresh lime juice
1   cup beer
        Lime slice

Stir the lime juice into the beer. Garnish with the lime slice.

❧ RUM IN THE DARK ❧

10   ounces beer
1   ounce dark rum

Combine both ingredients on the rocks, stirring well.

❧ DEW DROP ❧

3   ounces beer
2   ounces tequila
1   ounce Bacardi Dark Rum
1   ounce ouzo
        Mountain Dew

Combine all ingredients, except the Mountain Dew, in a tall glass. Top with the Mountain Dew.

❧ THE BIG O ❧

1	ounce curacao
	Splash of orange juice
	Ice
12	ounces beer

Combine the curacao, orange juice, and ice in a shaker, shaking well. Add the shaker mixture to the beer, stirring well.

❧ LEMON TICKLER ❧

1	ounce cynar
1/3	ounce lemon syrup
12	ounces beer

Combine the cynar and lemon syrup in a frosted mug. Add the beer, filling the mug and stirring well.

❧ DAREDEVIL'S BREW ❧

4	ounces gin
3	ounces beer
	Ice

Combine all ingredients in a shaker, shaking well. Strain the liquid into a glass.

⋇⟨ HOUND DOG ⟩⋇

3	ounces vodka
12	ounces beer
4	ounces Southern Comfort

Combine all ingredients on the rocks, stirring well.

⋇⟨ TONGUE TINGLER ⟩⋇

2	ounces Everclear
2	ounces vodka
2	ounces gin
1	ounce dark rum
1	ounce peppermint schnapps
2	ounces beer
	Cola

Combine all ingredients, except the cola, on the rocks in a highball glass. Fill the remainder of the glass with the cola, stirring well.

"THERE CAN'T BE GOOD LIVING WHERE THERE IS NOT GOOD DRINKING."

Benjamin Franklin, American inventor and statesman

⟩ GRIZZLY ⟨

¼	ounce triple sec
¼	ounce rum
¼	ounce vodka
¼	ounce gin
¼	ounce tequila
¼	ounce bourbon
¼	ounce scotch
12	ounces beer
12	ounces stout of choice

Combine all ingredients, except the beer and stout, in a mug, stirring well. Fill the remainder of the mug with equal parts of the beer and stout.

⟩ BEER MIST ⟨

1½	ounces Irish Mist
16	ounces beer

Combine both ingredients, stirring well.

"I DrInk TO make OTHer PeOPLe InTeresTIng."

George Jean Nathan, *American drama critic and editor*

❀❧ SKIP & GO NAKED ☙❀

1	ounce gin
2	ounces sour mix
	Beer

Stir together the gin and sour mix in a Collins glass filled with ice. Fill the remainder of the glass with the beer, stirring lightly.

❀❧ BEER MIMOSA ☙❀

4	ounces beer
4	ounces orange juice
	Splash of champagne

Pour the beer into a champagne glass. Add the orange juice, stirring well. Top with the champagne.

❀❧ BLUE MOON ☙❀

1	ounce vodka
2	teaspoons blue curacao
	Beer

Pour the vodka and blue curacao into a Pilsner glass. Fill the remainder of the glass with the beer. Stir gently.

❊{ FIRE & ICE }❊

5	ounces vodka
1½	ounces Fire and Ice
¼	cup beer
½	cup cola

Combine all ingredients on the rocks, stirring well.

❊{ THE O. P. }❊

1	ounce Malibu Rum
1	ounce peach schnapps
	Orange juice
	Pineapple juice
1	teaspoon beer
	Pineapple chunks
	Cherries
	Orange slice

Combine the rum and peach schnapps in a shaker, shaking well. Strain the mixture into a Collins glass filled with crushed ice. Pour in equal amounts of each juice. Top with the beer. Garnish by alternating the pineapple chunks and cherries on a pick and placing it along with the orange slice on the side of the glass.

❊⟩ SOUTHERN JACK ⟨❊

1	cup Southern Comfort
1	cup Jack Daniel's Whiskey
16	ounces beer

Combine all ingredients on the rocks, stirring well.

❊⟩ BEER CINNER ⟨❊

2	parts cinnamon schnapps (chilled)
1	part beer
	Splash of grenadine
	Cinnamon stick

Pour the cinnamon schnapps into a glass followed by the beer on the rocks. Top with the grenadine and add the cinnamon stick as a stir.

❊⟩ BEER JAMMER ⟨❊

1	shot rum
12	ounces beer
2	tablespoons lime juice

Add the rum to the beer in a frosted glass. Add the lime juice, stirring well.

❧ EEKING MONKEY ❧

3	shots 151 proof rum
4	shots spiced rum
1	ounce lime juice
1	ounce lemon juice
1	ounce papaya juice
2	ounces orange juice
3	ounces coconut milk
	Crushed ice
4	ounces beer
	Shredded coconut
	Papaya chunks
	Lime slice
	Lemon slice

Combine the rum and spiced rum in a shaker, shaking well. Stir in the juices, coconut milk, and ice, shaking well. Add the mixture to the beer, stirring well. Top with the shredded coconut. Garnish with the papaya chunks on a pick and place the lime and lemon slices on the side of the glass.

❧ LOVE POTION #7 ❧

	Splash of grenadine
2/3	glass beer
1/3	glass 7-Up

Add each ingredient to a glass in the above order over the rocks, stirring well.

❊⟩ BEERTINI ⟨❊

3	parts dry vermouth
3	parts sweet vermouth
3	parts gin
3	parts whiskey
8	parts beer
1	drop blue curacao
1	drop red vodka

Combine the vermouths, gin, and whiskey on the rocks in a martini glass. Add the beer followed by the blue curacao and red vodka.

❊⟩ HANGOVER ⟨❊

2	ounces vodka
3	ounces beer
4	ounces tomato juice
	Salt to taste
	Seasoned salt to taste
	Celery rib

Combine all ingredients, stirring well. Garnish with the celery.

"You're not drunk if you can lie on the floor without holding on."

Dean Martin, American singer and actor

⋅⟩ SOUR MOMMA ⟨⋅

1	ounce gin
1	ounce vodka
1	ounce grenadine
1	ounce sour mix
	Beer

Combine the gin, vodka, grenadine, and sour mix in a shaker, shaking well. Pour the mixture into a Collins glass filled with ice, filling about half to three fourths of the glass. Fill the remainder of the glass with the beer.

⋅⟩ BEER BENDER ⟨⋅

1	shot vodka
1/2	shot gin
2	ounces Gatorade
4	ounces Crown Royal
1	teaspoon salt
	Splash of lemon juice
6	ounces beer

Combine all ingredients on the rocks, stirring well.

❧{ BEER CRUSH }❧

12	ounces whiskey
12	ounces beer
12	ounces frozen lemonade concentrate
1	cup crushed ice
	Lemon slices

Combine all ingredients in a blender, blending well. Garnish each glass with a lemon slice.

❧{ SOUR PUSS }❧

1½	ounces amaretto
1	teaspoon beer
3	ounces sour mix
	Splash of Sprite

Combine the amaretto, beer, and sour mix in a glass filled with ice. Top with the Sprite, stirring well.

"Drink and dance and laugh and lie,
Love, the reeling midnight through,
For tomorrow we shall die!
(But, alas, we never do.)"

Dorothy Parker, American writer and poet

⁂{ TWIST & SHOUT }⁂

1	ounce vodka
2	ounces lemon soda
	Beer to taste
	Cola to taste

Combine the vodka and lemon soda, filling half of a frosted glass. Add the beer and cola as desired.

⁂{ CRANBERRY BEER }⁂

12	ounces beer
1	ounce cranberry juice

Combine both ingredients on the rocks, stirring well.

⁂{ AFTER DINNER MINT }⁂

1/3	part cognac
1/3	part crème de menthe
1/3	part beer
	Ice (add green food coloring when making the ice)

Combine all ingredients in a shaker, shaking well, and then pour into a glass.

ᗖ GRAND DAME ᗕ

½	ounce vodka
½	ounce gin
½	ounce rum
½	ounce Grand Marnier
¼	ounce Tia Maria
¼	ounce Kahlua
1	ounce sour mix
	Splash of cranberry juice
	Crushed ice
	Beer draft foam

Combine all of the alcohol, except the beer draft foam. Add the sour mix. Add the cranberry juice and crushed ice, stirring well. Top with the foam from the beer draft.

ᗖ THE ORIGINAL BEER MARGARITA ᗕ

1	pitcher ice
12	ounces frozen limeade concentrate
12	ounces beer
12	ounces tequila
3	splashes margarita mix
¼	cup salt
	Lime slices

Pour the ice into a blender until it is three fourths full. Add the limeade, beer, and tequila, blending until smooth. Add the margarita mix. Salt the rims of the margarita glasses. Pour the mixture into the glasses and garnish with the lime slices.

❖⟩ RED, WHITE, & BLUE ⟨❖

6	ounces beer
½	ounce blueberry brandy
2	ounces peach schnapps
1	ounce vodka
½	ounce Everclear
	Crushed ice

Combine all ingredients, stirring well.

❖⟩ APPLE TREE CIDER ⟨❖

8	ounces beer
8	ounces apple cider

Combine both ingredients, stirring well.

❖⟩ VOLCANO ⟨❖

2	parts beer
2	parts coconut rum
1	part vodka
1	part triple sec
2	parts melon liqueur

Combine all ingredients on the rocks, stirring well.

❖{ BEER GYPSY }❖

2	parts Jagermeister
1	part gin
1½	parts Drambuie
1	part Bailey's Irish Cream
	Beer
	Crème de menthe

Combine the Jagermeister, gin, Drambuie, and Bailey's Irish Cream on the rocks. Top with equal amounts of the beer and crème de menthe.

❖{ SCREWDRIVER }❖

2	ounces vodka
8	ounces orange juice
12	ounces beer

Combine the vodka and orange juice on the rocks, stirring well. Stir in the beer.

"WHEN WE DRINK, WE GET DRUNK. WHEN WE GET DRUNK, WE FALL ASLEEP. WHEN WE FALL ASLEEP, WE COMMIT NO SIN. WHEN WE COMMIT NO SIN, WE GO TO HEAVEN. SOOOOO, LET'S ALL GET DRUNK, AND GO TO HEAVEN."

Brian O'Rourke, Irish Lord

❧ GOODNIGHT, SWEETHEART ☙

1	gallon beer
8	ounces honey
	Pepper

In a saucepan, combine the beer and honey, stirring and heating the mixture until the honey is dissolved. Place the pepper in an infuser and steep it in the mixture overnight. Serve the drink hot in mugs.

❧ CREAMY SODA ☙

| 1 | part beer |
| 1 | part cream soda |

Combine both ingredients on the rocks, stirring well.

❧ CHULITRO ☙

1½	ounces pisco
2	ice cubes
	Cola (to fill the glass)
	Dash of beer
	Lemon juice to taste

Layer the ingredients in the above order.

❧ BEER DAIQUIRI ❧

½	cup ice
5	ounces beer
½	ounce tequila
½	ounce light rum
3	ounces strawberry daiquiri mix
3	ounces margarita mix
	Fresh strawberries

Pour the ingredients (including some of the fresh strawberries) into a blender in the above order, blending until frothy. Garnish with the fresh strawberries on a pick.

❧ TEQUILA SUNRISE ❧

4	ounces tequila
1	ounce rum
1	ounce vodka
8	ounces beer

Pour 2 ounces of the tequila over ice into a shaker and shake. Add the rum and vodka, and shake. Add this mixture to the beer. Add the rest of the tequila, pouring it over the back of a spoon.

⚜{ BORDER CROSSING }⚜

2	ounces tequila
	Dash of bitters
	Beer

Combine the tequila and bitters in a highball glass, stirring well. Fill the remainder of the glass with the beer.

⚜{ A BIERE }⚜

1	ounce Amer Picon
1/3	ounce lemon syrup
	Beer

Combine the Amer Picon and lemon syrup in a mug. Fill the remainder of the mug with the beer, stirring well.

"I FEEL SORRY FOR PEOPLE WHO DON'T DRINK.
WHEN THEY WAKE UP IN THE MORNING, THAT'S
AS GOOD AS THEY'RE GOING TO FEEL ALL DAY."

Frank Sinatra, American singer

❊꜀ CLAM'S EYE ꜀❊

	Pinch of salt
	Dash of lemon juice
	Pinch of pepper
6	ounces clamato juice
6	ounces beer
1	ounce Tabasco sauce (or to taste)

Combine the salt, lemon juice, and pepper. Add the clamato juice. Slowly add the beer. Add the Tabasco sauce. Serve on the rocks.

❊꜀ DREAMSICLE ꜀❊

1	ounce amaretto
4	ounces beer
4	ounces orange juice
2	drops sugar syrup
	Crushed ice

Combine all ingredients, stirring well.

"WHO-ever makes a poor beer is tranferred to the dung hill."

City of Danzig edict, 11th Century

⁕{ HEAD TRIP }⁕

1	ounce Everclear
2	tablespoons beer
2	ounces butterscotch schnapps
	Root beer to taste

Combine all ingredients on the rocks, stirring well.

⁕{ BUTTER BEER }⁕

10	ounces beer
1	ounce butterscotch schnapps

Combine both ingredients, stirring well.

⁕{ HOTTIE }⁕

7	ounces clamato juice (room temperature)
12	ounces beer
	Celery salt to taste
	Tabasco sauce to taste
	Worchestershire sauce to taste
	Celery rib

Shake the clamato juice and then pour it into a Pilsner glass. Pour the beer down the side of the glass. Garnish with the seasonings to taste and the celery.

⁍{ BEER-A-LADE }⁌

4	ounces beer
5	ounces Gatorade (lemon-lime)
1	drop Tabasco sauce
	Maple syrup to taste

Combine the beer and Gatorade on the rocks, stirring well. Add the Tabasco Sauce. Slowly add the maple syrup to taste.

⁍{ SOUTHERN AMARETTO }⁌

2	ounces amaretto
3	ounces Southern Comfort
6	ounces beer

Combine all ingredients in a frosted glass, stirring well.

"The roots and herbes beaten and put into new ale or beer and daily drunk, cleareth, strengtheneth and quickeneth the sight of the eyes."

Nicholas Culpeper, English botanist, herbalist, physician, and astrologer

CHAPTER 22

Chuggers

❊⟨ BOILERMAKER ⟩❊

| 2 | ounces whiskey |
| 10 | ounces beer |

Pour the whiskey into a shot glass and the beer into a mug. Drop the shot glass into the mug and chug.

❊⟨ WIDOWMAKER ⟩❊

| 1 | ounce vodka |
| 16 | ounces beer |

Pour the vodka into a shot glass and the beer into a mug. Drop the shot glass into the mug and chug.

❊⟨ KAHLUA SHOOT OUT ⟩❊

| 1 | ounce Kahlua |
| 12 | ounces beer |

Pour the Kahlua into a shot glass and the beer into a mug. Drop the shot glass into the mug and chug.

❧ DEPTH CHARGE ❧

| 1 | ounce Drambuie |
| 12 | ounces beer |

Pour the Drambuie into a shot glass and the beer into a mug. Drop the shot glass into the mug and chug.

❧ SAMBUCA ❧

| 1 | ounce sambuca |
| 12 | ounces beer |

Pour the sambuca into a shot glass and the beer into a mug. Drop the shot glass into the mug and chug.

❧ WOODPECKER ❧

10	ounces Mountain Dew
2	ounces vodka
12	ounces beer
	Dash of honey

Combine all ingredients, stirring well. Chug.

❧ TEQUILA SKY ROCKET ❧

1	ounce tequila
12	ounces beer
1	lime

Pour the tequila into a shot glass and the beer into a mug. Drop the shot glass into the mug, squeeze the lime on top, and chug.

❧ BEER BEER CHUGGER ❧

1	ounce root beer schnapps
8	ounces beer

Pour the root beer schnapps into a shot glass and the beer into a mug. Drop the shot glass into the mug and chug.

❧ THE MOULIN SLIDER ❧

1/2	ounce absinthe
1/2	ounce cinnamon schnapps
12	ounces beer

Pour the absinthe and cinnamon schnapps into a shot glass and the beer into a mug. Drink a quarter of the beer, drop the shot glass into the mug, and chug.

❧ DANCIN' MOMMA ☙

½	ounce dark rum
½	ounce tequila
6	ounces beer

Pour the dark rum and tequila into a shot glass, stirring well. Pour the beer into a mug. Drop the shot glass into the mug and chug.

❧ LUNCH BOX ☙

½	ounce amaretto
4	ounces beer
½	ounce orange juice

Pour the amaretto into a shot glass. Pour the beer and orange juice into a mug, stirring well. Drop the shot glass into the mug and chug.

"WE'LL RAISE UP OUR GLASSES AGAINST EVIL FORCES SINGIN', 'WHISKEY FOR MY MEN, AND BEER FOR OUR HORSES.'"

Toby Keith and Willie Nelson, American country music singers, "Whiskey for My Men"

⁘⟩ THE REBEL'S YELL ⟨⁘

¾	ounce Rebel Yell 101
	Bacardi Limon
6	ounces beer
	Splash of cola

Pour the Rebel Yell 101 into a shot glass and then fill the rest of the shot glass with the Bacardi Limon. Pour the beer into a mug, filling the mug halfway, and add the cola. Drop the shot glass into the mug and chug.

⁘⟩ HOT SAKE BEER BOMB ⟨⁘

1	ounce hot sake
6	ounces beer

Pour the sake into a shot glass and the beer into a mug. Drop the shot glass into the mug and chug.

⁘⟩ STRAWBERRY JOLT ⟨⁘

1½	ounces strawberry liqueur
12	ounces beer

Pour the strawberry liqueur into a shot glass and the beer into a mug. Drop the shot glass into the mug and chug.

⸭❴ BUCKSHOT ❵⸭

1	ounce Midori
½	glass beer
½	glass 7-Up

Pour the Midori into a shot glass. Pour the beer into a mug followed by the 7-Up. Drop the shot glass into the mug and chug.

⸭❴ GREEN GOBLIN ❵⸭

1	part gin
1	part sweet vermouth
1	part lime juice
1	part melon liqueur
16	ounces beer

Pour all ingredients, except the beer, into a shot glass. Pour the beer into a mug. Drop the shot glass into the mug and chug.

⸭❴ BEER BLITZ ❵⸭

⅓	ounce amaretto
⅔	ounce root beer schnapps
12	ounces beer

Pour the amaretto and root beer schnapps into a shot glass and the beer into a mug. Drop the shot glass into the mug and chug.

❧ HUNTING CAMP SPECIAL ❧

1	shot 151 proof rum
1	shot tequila
1	shot bourbon
1	shot vodka
2	shots Wild Turkey
6	ounces beer

Combine all ingredients, stirring well. Chug.

❧ VODKA CHUGGER ❧

3	ounces beer
1½	ounces vodka
	Dash of grenadine

Combine all ingredients, stirring well. Chug.

❧ IRISH CAR BOMB ❧

¾	ounce Irish whiskey
¾	ounce Irish cream
6	ounces beer

Pour the whiskey and Irish cream into a shot glass and the beer into a mug. Drop the shot glass into the mug and chug.

CHAPTER 23

Shots
&
Shooters

❧ TROPICAL NECTAR ❧

⅓	ounce Midori
⅙	ounce beer
⅓	ounce pineapple juice
⅕	ounce lemonade
	Orange juice to taste

Combine all ingredients in a shot glass, stirring well.

❧ GIN BLAST ❧

1	ounce gin
½	ounce beer

Combine both ingredients in a shot glass, stirring well.

❧ SWEETIE ❧

4	parts Drambuie
2	parts vodka
2	parts beer

Combine all ingredients in a shot glass, stirring well.

⁖⦃ IRISH SETTER ⦄⁖

¼	shot vodka
½	shot Bailey's Irish Cream
	Splash of beer

Layer the vodka and Bailey's Irish Cream in a shot glass. Top with the beer.

⁖⦃ ATOMIC DIVA ⦄⁖

7	ounces beer
17	ounces aquavit

Combine the beer and aquavit in a pitcher, stirring well. Serve as shots.

⁖⦃ HONEY DROP ⦄⁖

2	parts tequila
1	part beer
	Juice from 1 lime
½	teaspoon honey

Combine the tequila, beer, and lime juice in a shot glass, mixing well. Pour the honey in a teaspoon. Drop the teaspoon of honey into the shot glass and drink quickly.

❊❴ BEER & JELL-O SHOT ❵❊

3	cups water
3	3-ounce packages Jell-O of choice
2	cups beer

Boil the water and add the Jell-O, stirring well until the Jell-O is dissolved. Add the beer, continuing to stir well. Pour the mixture into plastic shot glasses. Chill until firm and serve.

"Take a gallon of strong stale beer, one pound of anchovies washed from the pickle, a pound of shallots peeled, half an ounce of mace, half an ounce of cloves, a quarter of an ounce of whole pepper, three or four large races of ginger, two quarts of large mushroom flaps rubbed to pieces; cover all these close, and let it simmer til it is half wasted, then strain it through a flannel bag; let it stand til it is quite cold, then bottle it. You may carry it to the Indies. A spoonful of this to a pound of fresh butter melted makes a fine fish-sauce, or in the room of gravy sauce. The stronger and staler the beer is, the better the catchup will be."

Hannah Glasse, Recipe for sea captains from *The Art of Cookery Made Plain and Easy,* 1796

CHAPTER 24

Chasers

❧ NIGHT CRAWLER ❧

½	ounce tequila
½	ounce triple sec
½	ounce Jack Daniel's Whiskey
8	ounces beer

Combine the tequila, triple sec, and whiskey in a shot glass. Down the shot and chase it with the beer.

❧ PICKLED VODKA ❧

1	ounce vodka
½	ounce pickle juice of choice
8	ounces beer

Combine the vodka and pickle juice in a shot glass, stirring well. Down the shot and chase it with the beer.

❧ WILD TURKEY CHASE ❧

1	ounce Bacardi 151 Proof Rum
1	ounce Wild Turkey
8	ounces beer

Combine the rum and Wild Turkey in a shot glass, stirring well. Down the shot and chase it with the beer.

❦ HOOT & HOLLER ❦

½	ounce triple sec
½	ounce Kahlua
½	ounce tequila
	Ice
6	ounces beer

Combine the triple sec, Kahlua, tequila, and ice in a shaker, shaking well. Strain the mixture into a shot glass. Down the shot and chase it with the beer.

❦ SHOOTING STARS ❦

1	ounce Jagermeister
1	ounce Jack Daniel's Whiskey
1	ounce Everclear
1	ounce After Shock
8	ounces beer

Pour each of the 1 ounce drinks into a separate shot glass. Down each shot separately in the order above and chase them with the beer.

"WHY DO I DRINK? SO THAT I CAN WRITE POETRY."

Jim Morrison, American singer

❧ DRUNKEN LEPRECHAUN ❧

1/3	ounce Bailey's Irish Cream
2/3	ounce crème de menthe
1	ounce beer

Combine the Bailey's Irish Cream and crème de menthe in a shot glass, stirring well. Down the shot and chase it with the beer.

❧ HOT BALLERS ❧

20	drops Tabasco sauce
1	shot tequila
1	shot peppermint schnapps
8	ounces beer

Pour the Tabasco sauce, tequila, and peppermint schnapps into 3 different shot glasses. Down each shot separately in the order above and chase them with the beer.

"IF YOU DRINK, DON'T DRIVE. DON'T EVEN PUTT."

Dean Martin, American singer and actor

❧ BALL HOOTER ❧

1	part tequila
1	part peppermint schnapps
	Ice
8	ounces beer

Combine the tequila, peppermint schnapps, and ice in a shaker, shaking well. Strain the mixture into a shot glass. Down the shot and chase it with the beer.

❧ BEER BABBLER ❧

½	ounce amaretto
½	ounce Southern Comfort
8	ounces beer

Combine the amaretto and Southern Comfort in a shot glass. Down the shot and chase it with the beer.

❧ AUNT REGGIE ❧

1	shot whiskey
8	ounces beer

Down the shot and chase it with the beer.

❖{ SPINAL TAP }❖

½	ounce Green Chartreuse
½	ounce Bacardi 151 Proof Rum
8	ounces beer

Combine the Green Chartreuse and rum in a shot glass, stirring well. Down the shot and chase it with the beer.

"LIFE AIN'T ALL BEER AND SKITTLES, AND MORE'S THE PITY."

George DuMaurier, Paris-born, British author and cartoonist

CHAPTER 25

Party Punches

❧ CITRUS SUNSATION PUNCH ❧

2	cups sugar
2	cups water
6	lemons, juiced with the peels sliced
1	cup orange juice
24	ounces beer
	7-Up (frozen into ice cubes)
	Orange slices

Combine the sugar and water. Bring to a boil. Add the lemon peels, remove from heat, and cover for 5 minutes. Remove the peels. Add the lemon and orange juices. Stir well. Pour into a pitcher and refrigerate for several hours. Stir in the beer and 7-Up ice cubes just before serving the punch. Garnish with the orange slices.

❧ BEER-TANG ❧

10	ounces beer
12	ounces orange juice
1	quart ginger ale
2	tablespoons lime juice
3	ounces sugar
	Lemonade (frozen into ice cubes)

Combine all ingredients, stirring well.

⁘{ PINK PUNCH BUG }⁘

1	12-ounce can pink lemonade concentrate
12	ounces water
12	ounces vodka
12	ounces beer
	Pink lemonade (frozen into ice cubes)

Pour the lemonade into a gallon pitcher. Add the water and vodka. Stir well. Add the beer and pink lemonade ice cubes. Mix well.

⁘{ GINGER PUNCH }⁘

1½	ounces gin
12	ounces beer
12	ounces ginger beer
	Juice from ½ lemon
	Splash of soda water
	Ginger ale (frozen into ice cubes)

Combine all ingredients, stirring well.

"Ale, man, ale's the stuff to drink
For fellows whom it hurts to think."

A.E. Housman, English poet

❧ NEW YEAR'S PUNCH ❧

1	gallon vodka
1	gallon + 16 ounces beer
2	liters Sprite
1	19-ounce can powdered lemonade mix
	Sprite (frozen into ice cubes)
	Cherries (frozen inside the ice cubes)
	Orange rinds (frozen inside the ice cubes)
	Green grapes (frozen inside the ice cubes)

Combine all ingredients, stirring well.

❧ TOM & JERRY BEER PUNCH ❧

24	ounces beer
1/2	cup sugar
1	cinnamon stick
1/4	teaspoon grated nutmeg
4	eggs
1/4	cup rum
1/4	cup brandy
1	teaspoon pure vanilla extract

Combine the beer, sugar, cinnamon stick, and nutmeg. Heat the mixture until the sugar dissolves. Lightly beat the eggs while slowly adding the rum and brandy. Remove the beer mixture from the heat and remove the cinnamon stick. Stir in the egg mixture followed by the vanilla. Serve hot.

›{ SOUR PATCH PUNCH }‹

1	cup sugar
1	cup water
3	lemons, juiced with the zest removed and saved
½	cup chilled grapefruit juice
12	ounces beer
	Squirt (frozen into ice cubes)
	Several lemon slices
	Several cherries

Combine the sugar and water and bring to a boil over a high heat. Stir until the sugar is dissolved. Add the lemon zest and remove the mixture from the heat. Cover and let cool for 10 minutes. Remove the lemon zest and allow the mixture to cool to room temperature. Add the lemon and grapefruit juices to the sugar mixture. Chill for 2 to 3 hours. Stir in the beer and Squirt ice cubes before serving. Garnish the servings with the lemon slices and cherries.

"WHISKEY'S TOO ROUGH,
CHAMPAGNE COSTS TOO MUCH,
VODKA PUTS MY MOUTH IN GEAR.
I HOPE THIS REFRAIN,
WILL HELP ME EXPLAIN,
AS A MATTER OF FACT,
I LIKE BEER."

Tom T. Hall, American country music singer

❊⟩ LEMON PUNCH ⟨❊

1	6-ounce can lemonade concentrate
36	ounces water
	Lemonade (frozen into ice cubes)
24	ounces beer
1½	cups rum
	Lemon slices
	Cherries
	Sprigs of mint

Combine the lemonade and water, stirring well. Pour the lemonade into a punch bowl filled with the lemonade ice cubes. Add the beer and rum, stirring well. Garnish with the lemon slices, cherries, and sprigs of mint.

❊⟩ 4TH OF JULY PARADE PUNCH ⟨❊

1	gallon vodka
2	quarts beer
4	6-ounce cans lemonade concentrate
4	cups water
2	quarts fruit punch
	Blueberry Kool-Aid (frozen into a star-shaped ice mold)
	Fresh blueberries (frozen inside the ice mold)

Combine all ingredients, except the ice mold, stirring well. Pour the punch into a punch bowl and add the star-shaped blueberry ice mold.

❧ VINEYARD PUNCH ❧

1	quart vodka
½	gallon red wine
1	quart ginger ale
12	ounces beer
	Ginger ale (frozen into ice cubes)
	Red grapes (frozen inside the ice cubes)

Combine all ingredients, except the beer and ginger ale ice, stirring well. Add the beer. Add the ginger ale ice. Stir well.

❧ FREEDOM PUNCH ❧

1	fifth vodka
2	quarts + 8 ounces beer
2	scoops powdered lemonade
	Water to taste
	Sugar to taste
	Ice
	Raspberries (frozen inside the ice cubes)
	Lemon slices

Combine all ingredients, except the lemon slices, stirring well. Garnish with the lemon slices.

❧ ORIGINAL FRUIT PUNCH ❧

1⅔	cups rum
12	ounces beer
4	cups orange juice
3	cups pineapple juice
2	cups Ocean Spray Juice
	Splash of banana liqueur
	Ice
	Pineapple chunks
	Banana slices
	Cherries
	Papaya chunks
	Orange slices

Combine all ingredients, except the fruit, stirring well. Add all of the fruit, allowing it to float in the punch bowl.

"'Did you ever taste beer?'
'I had a sip of it once,' said the small servant.
'Here's a state of things!' cried Mr. Swiveller . . .
'She never tasted it — it can't be tasted in a sip!'"
                    Charles Dickens, English author, *Ye Olde Curiosity Shop*

⁖{ CLOUD 9 }⁖

1	quart vodka
1	quart brandy
1	quart gin
1	quart light rum
1	quart Lambrusco
3	gallons fruit punch
	Ice
2	quarts + 8 ounces beer

Combine all ingredients, adding the beer last and stirring well.

⁖{ GARDEN OF EDEN PUNCH }⁖

1/4	cup (1/2 stick) butter
1	cup sugar
1/2	teaspoon grated nutmeg
1/2	teaspoon ground ginger
8	apples, sliced
2	quarts beer

Melt the butter. Add the sugar, stirring well. Add the nutmeg and ginger, continuing to stir. Place the apple slices in the mixture. Top with the beer. Slowly heat and serve warm.

❉{ BERRY PICKING PUNCH }❉

1	fifth vodka
3	12-ounce bottles beer
2	cans fruit punch
	Ice (create using an ice mold)
	Strawberries (frozen inside the ice mold)
	Blueberries (frozen inside the ice mold)
	Blackberries (frozen inside the ice mold)
	Raspberries (frozen inside the ice mold)
3	lemons, sliced
3	limes, sliced

Combine the vodka, beer, fruit punch, and ice mold. Garnish with the fruit slices. The berries may also be used to garnish the punch.

❉{ MIDNIGHT MOON & FIDDLE PUNCH }❉

16	ounces 151 proof rum
16	ounces blackberry brandy
12	ounces beer
1	12-ounce can cola
1	12-ounce can orange soda
1	12-ounce can 7-Up
32	ounces pineapple juice
	Ice

Combine all ingredients, stirring well.

❧ BEACH PARTY PUNCH ❧

4	ounces rum
4	ounces vodka
4	ounces amaretto
4	ounces gin
24	ounces beer
1	12-ounce can Sprite
8	ounces orange juice
8	ounces pineapple juice
	Ice

Combine all ingredients, stirring well.

❧ WEDDING PUNCH ❧

7	cups vodka
7	cups gin
7	cups rum
13½	quarts beer
10	quarts pink lemonade
	Pink lemonade (frozen into ice cubes)

Combine all ingredients, stirring well.

⁎{ ORANGE FIZZ }⁎

8	ounces gin
11	ounces beer
16	ounces orange soda
	Ice
	Orange slices

Combine all ingredients, except the orange slices in a blender. Blend for 3 minutes. Garnish each serving with an orange slice.

⁎{ MALIBU RUM RUN }⁎

12	ounces beer
2½	ounces Malibu Rum
1½	cups orange juice
7	ounces 7-Up
2	splashes lemon juice
9	ounces beer
6	ounces Mountain Dew
1	ounce Malibu Rum
	Orange juice (frozen into an ice mold)
	Lemon slices

Combine the 12 ounces of beer, 2½ ounces of rum, orange juice, 7-Up, and lemon juice, stirring well. Combine the 9 ounces of beer, Mountain Dew, and 1 ounce of rum, stirring well. Combine both mixtures, stirring well. Pour the punch into a punch bowl filled with the orange juice ice mold. Garnish each glass with a lemon slice.

ᛮ{ POLKA PUNCH }ᛮ

	Crushed ice
12	ounces beer
2	ounces vodka
2	ounces Southern Comfort
2	ounces sloe gin
2	ounces gin
2	ounces grenadine
	7-Up
	Orange juice

Put a layer of crushed ice at the bottom of a pitcher. Add the beer followed by the other ingredients. Top off the remainder of the pitcher with equal amounts of 7-Up and orange juice. Stir well.

ᛮ{ PEACHY PUNCH }ᛮ

2	cups vodka
12	ounces peach schnapps
36	ounces beer
1	quart water
6	ounces powdered orange Tang mix (or more to taste)
	Ice

Combine all ingredients, stirring well.

❧ FRIENDSHIP PUNCH ❧

40	ounces beer
12	ounces ginger ale
¼	shot vodka
¼	shot light rum
½	shot amaretto
	Ice

Combine all ingredients, stirring well.

❧ SUN-KISSED PUNCH ❧

1	quart + 8 ounces beer
34	ounces vodka
2	gallons orange juice
	Orange juice (frozen into an ice mold and crushed)

Combine all ingredients, stirring well.

"DRINKING WHEN WE ARE NOT THIRSTY AND
MAKING LOVE AT ALL SEASONS, MADAM: THAT
IS ALL THERE IS TO DISTINGUISH US FROM
OTHER ANIMALS."

Pierre de Beaumarchais, French playwright

❧{ POWER PUNCH }❧

12	12-ounce bottles beer
2	cans pink lemonade concentrate
13	ounces Absolut Vodka
13	ounces Canadian whisky
	Pink lemonade (frozen into ice cubes)

Combine all ingredients, stirring well.

❧{ TRICK OR TREAT PUNCH }❧

1	gallon After Shock
11	ounces beer
12	ounces Jack Daniel's Orange Whiskey
10	ounces sparkling wine
3	ounces 7-Up
½	ounce apple juice
1	12-ounce can Dr. Pepper
4	ounces grenadine
	Dr. Pepper (frozen into ice cubes)
	Gummy worms
	Candy corn
	Jolly Ranchers

Combine all ingredients, except the candy, stirring well. Garnish with the gummy worms, candy corn, Jolly Ranchers, and any other candy of choice. Serve in a punch bowl placed in a large hollowed-out pumpkin or a plastic pumpkin.

❄} HOLIDAY EGG NOG {❄

3	eggs, separated
½	cup sugar
2	cups milk OR 1 gallon prepared egg nog
12	ounces beer
¼	cup brandy or bourbon
1	cup whipped cream
	Grated nutmeg

Beat the egg yolks with ¼ cup of the sugar until the mixture is thick. Stir in the milk, beer, and brandy. Beat the egg whites until foamy. Beat in the remaining ¼ cup of sugar until stiff peaks form. Fold the egg whites into the egg yolk mixture. OR, combine the prepared egg nog, beer, and brandy, stirring well.

Chill. Before serving, fold in the whipped cream. Top with more whipped cream and the nutmeg.

❄} YARD OF FLANNEL {❄

34	ounces beer
4	eggs
3	tablespoons sugar
½	teaspoon grated nutmeg
½	teaspoon ground cinnamon
½	cup Haitian Rum
	Boiling water

Heat the beer in a saucepan over a low heat. Beat the eggs with the other ingredients and pour the mixture into a pitcher. Pour the beer into the egg mixture, stirring until frothy.

ᵉᵗ STRAWBERRY SLUSH ᵗᵉ

1	.14-ounce package strawberry Kool-Aid
3	cups sugar
6	ounces frozen orange juice
4½	cups warm water
1	10-ounce package strawberries
1	cup vodka
½	cup beer
	Ginger ale to taste

Dissolve the Kool-Aid, sugar, and orange juice in the warm water. Add the other ingredients, except the ginger ale, stirring well. Freeze. To serve, scoop the slushy mixture into a glass and add the ginger ale to taste.

ᵉᵗ MOJO PUNCH ᵗᵉ

1	quart light rum
1	quart dark rum
16	ounces cherry brandy
1	quart + 8 ounces beer
5	cans 7-Up
4	quarts pineapple juice
2	or more bags of ice
	Cherries (to float in the punch)

Combine all ingredients, stirring well.

❧ MAY DAY SIMA ❧

1	gallon + 42 ounces water
5¼	ounces sugar
5¼	ounces brown sugar
5¼	ounces beer
1	lemon
2	teaspoons yeast
5	to 6 raisins per bottle
1	tablespoon sugar per bottle

Combine and boil the water, sugars, beer, and the yellow part of the lemon's peel. Let the mixture cool.

Peel the white part of the lemon's peel carefully and cut the fruit part of the lemon into small pieces and add to the mixture.

Dissolve the yeast in a bit of the mixture and then add it to the mixture. Put 5 to 6 raisins and 1 tablespoon of sugar into every bottle. Put the mixture into the bottles and close the bottles. Leave the sima in a cold place for a few days.

Sima is ready when the raisins float. Sima will keep in a cold place for 1 to 2 weeks.

❧ BOTTLE PUNCH ❧

40	ounces beer
1	quart Sunny Delight Orange Juice

Using bottles of beer, pour half of the beer out of each bottle and fill the remainder of each bottle with the orange juice. Shake and drink.

Be sure not to waste the beer you poured out of the bottle!

CHAPTER 26

Floats & Milkshakes

⁂{ ROOT BEER FLOAT }⁂

12	ounces beer
6	tablespoons vanilla ice cream
4	ounces root beer schnapps

Combine all ingredients in a blender, blending until smooth.

⁂{ BERRY FLOAT }⁂

12	ounces beer
3	scoops strawberry ice cream
	Whipped cream
	Cherries or strawberries

Combine the beer and ice cream. Garnish with the whipped cream and cherries or strawberries.

⁂{ TRIPLE MINT FLOAT }⁂

12	ounces beer
3	scoops mint-chocolate chip ice cream
1	teaspoon crème de menthe
	Chocolate mint candy (Andes), shaved
	Sprig of mint

Combine the beer, ice cream, and crème de menthe in a blender, blending until smooth. Top with the chocolate mint candy shavings and garnish with the sprig of mint.

⁘⟩ CHOCOLATE BEERSHAKE ⟨⁘

3	ounces beer
	Splash of Jack Daniel's Whiskey
2	cups Kahlua
2	cups milk
1	cup tonic water
1	quart chocolate ice cream

Combine all ingredients in a blender, blending until smooth.

⁘⟩ VANILLA CREAM FLOAT ⟨⁘

½	glass beer
½	glass vanilla ice cream
	Whipped cream
	Small marshmallows
	Cherry

Pour the beer over the ice cream. Freeze the mixture for several hours until slushy. To serve, top with the whipped cream, marshmallows, and cherry.

"WHEN I READ ABOUT THE EVILS OF DRINKING,
I GAVE UP READING."

Henny Youngman, British-American comedian and violinist

❊{ COCONUT FLOAT }❊

2	tablespoons coconut rum
½	glass beer
½	glass vanilla ice cream
	Shredded coconut
	Whipped cream
	Cherry

Pour the rum and then the beer over the ice cream. Freeze the mixture for several hours until slushy. To serve, top with the shredded coconut, whipped cream, and cherry.

❊{ IRISH CREAM FLOAT }❊

2	ounces Bailey's Irish Cream
¾	ounce vodka
	Root beer to taste
	Beer to taste
	Vanilla ice cream to taste

Combine the Bailey's Irish Cream and vodka. Add the root beer and beer, but do not mix. Add the ice cream.

"CANDY IS DANDY BUT, LIQUOR IS QUICKER."

Ogden Nash, American poet

CHAPTER 27

Beer on Fire

⁂{ FLAMING DOCTOR PEPPER }⁂

³⁄₄	ounce amaretto
¹⁄₄	ounce Bacardi 151 Proof Rum
¹⁄₂	cup beer

Combine the amaretto and rum in a shot glass. Pour the beer into a tall glass. Light the shot on fire and drop it into the glass of beer. Making sure that the flame is extinguished, chug.

Use extreme caution with the fire.

⁂{ FLAMEMAKER }⁂

| 2 | ounces Everclear |
| 12 | ounces beer |

Pour the Everclear into a shot glass and the beer into a tall glass. Light the shot on fire and drop it into the glass. Making sure that the flame is extinguished, chug.

Use extreme caution with the fire.

"There is nothing which has yet been contrived by man, by which so much happiness is produced as by a good tavern or inn."

Samuel Johnson, English author

⁛ᔶ CRAIG'S OUTHOUSE SLAMMER ᔷ⁛

1	ounce Everclear
3	ounces cola
2	ounces beer

Pour the Everclear into a shot glass. Combine the cola and beer in a tall glass, stirring well. Light the shot on fire and drop it into the glass. Making sure that the flame is extinguished, chug.

Use extreme caution with the fire.

⁛ᔶ BARN BURNER ᔷ⁛

32	ounces Everclear
6	ounces beer
16	ounces milk

Combine all ingredients in a pitcher, stirring well. Pour the mixture into tall glasses. Light the mixture on fire. Once the fire goes out, drink.

Use extreme caution with the fire.

"A WOMAN DROVE ME TO DRINK AND I DIDN'T EVEN HAVE THE DECENCY TO THANK HER."

W.C. Fields, American comedian

❧ BURNING BUSH ❧

1	ounce Hot Damn
1/2	glass beer
1/2	glass apple cider

Pour the Hot Damn into a shot glass. Pour the apple cider and beer into a tall glass. Light the shot on fire and drop it into the glass. Making sure that the flame is extinguished, chug.

Use extreme caution with the fire.

❧ BLAZING COMET ❧

1/2	ounce amaretto
1/2	ounce whiskey
	Dash of Everclear
8	ounces beer

Combine the amaretto and whiskey in a shot glass. Top the shot glass mixture with the Everclear. Pour the beer into a tall glass. Light the shot on fire and drop it into the glass of beer. Making sure that the flame is extinguished, chug.

Use extreme caution with the fire.

"THE PROBLEM WITH THE WORLD IS THAT EVERYONE IS A FEW DRINKS BEHIND."

Humphrey Bogart, American actor

❧ RASPBERRY BONFIRE ❧

³/₄	ounce Chambord Raspberry Liqueur
¹/₄	ounce Bacardi 151 Proof Rum
8	ounces beer

Layer the liqueur and rum in a shot glass. Pour the beer into a tall glass. Light the shot on fire and drop it into the glass of beer. Making sure that the flame is extinguished, chug.

Use extreme caution with the fire.

❧ COCONUT BONFIRE ❧

¹/₂	ounce amaretto
¹/₂	ounce coconut rum
8	ounces beer

Layer the amaretto and rum in a shot glass. Pour the beer into a tall glass. Light the shot on fire and drop it into the glass of beer. Making sure that the flame is extinguished, chug.

Use extreme caution with the fire.

"THE MAN THAT ISN'T JOLLY AFTER DRINKING IS JUST A DRIVELING IDIOT, TO MY THINKING."

Euripides, Greek tragedian

❧ FLAMING SAKE BOMB ❧

¾	ounce sake
¼	ounce Everclear
½	ounce Midori
16	ounces beer

Pour the sake into a shot glass and top it with the Everclear. Combine the Midori and beer in a tall glass. Light the shot on fire and drop it into the glass. Making sure that the flame is extinguished, chug.

Use extreme caution with the fire.

❧ TEQUILA SUNBURN ❧

1¼	ounces tequila
	Splash of Bacardi 151 Proof Rum
6	ounces beer

Pour the tequila into a shot glass and top it with the rum. Pour the beer into a tall glass. Light the shot on fire and drop it into the glass of beer. Making sure that the flame is extinguished, chug.

Use extreme caution with the fire.

"I went on a diet, swore off drinking and heavy eating, and in fourteen days I lost two weeks."

Joe E. Lewis, American comedian and singer

AFTERWORD

If you would like to learn more about beer history, types of beers, pairing food with beer, creating homebrews, beer trivia, the genre of collecting beer memorabilia called Breweriana, or just about anything else having to do with beer, I suggest you check out www.beerbooks.com. There, you will find books, magazines, videos, and much more on all things beer.

There are also many other very helpful web sites about these beer topics, as well as about beer festivals around the world, which you can access by typing "beer" into your favorite search engine. From the thousands of sites that will pop-up on your screen you'll once more see just what a living legend it is you're working with.

INDEX